A STROLL IN THE RAIN

Also by George Bradley

A Stroll in the Rain

NEW AND SELECTED POEMS

George Bradley

LOUISIANA STATE UNIVERSITY PRESS

BATON ROUGE

Published by Louisiana State University Press
lsupress.org

Manufactured in the United States of America
First printing

DESIGNER: Michelle A. Neustrom
TYPEFACE: Livory
PRINTER AND BINDER: Sheridan Books, Inc.

Poems from Of the Knowledge of Good and Evil, The Fire Fetched Down, and Some
Assembly Required are reprinted by arrangement with Alfred A. Knopf, an imprint
of The Knopf Doubleday Publishing Group, a division of Penguin Random House LLC.

COVER IMAGE: *A Spring Shower*, ca. 1790–1804, by Giovanni Domenico Tiepolo.
Courtesy the Cleveland Museum of Art. Purchase from the J. H. Wade Fund.

LIBRARY OF CONGRESS CATALOGING-IN-PUBLICATION DATA
Names: Bradley, George, 1953– author.
Title: A stroll in the rain : new and selected poems / George Bradley.
Description: Baton Rouge : Louisiana State University Press, [2021]
Identifiers: LCCN 2020056061 (print) | LCCN 2020056062 (ebook) | ISBN 978-0-8071-
7584-2 (cloth) | ISBN 978-0-8071-7562-0 (paperback) | ISBN 978-0-8071-7612-2 (pdf) |
ISBN 978-0-8071-7613-9 (epub)
Subjects: LCGFT: Poetry.
Classification: LCC PS3552.R227 S77 2021 (print) | LCC PS3552.R227 (ebook) |
DDC 811/.54—dc23
LC record available at https://lccn.loc.gov/2020056061
LC ebook record available at https://lccn.loc.gov/2020056062

ↄ

This book is dedicated to several people, living and dead, without whom the poems in it would not exist in anything like their present form: Richard Howard, Jay Clayton, Eleanor Ross Taylor, and Spencer Boyd. Friends and collaborators, they helped this work immeasurably, and I have long been grateful for their generous attention and useful advice.

CONTENTS

FROM

Terms to Be Met

1986

In Suspense

at the Verrazano Narrows Bridge

The composition of many particulars
Held the broad promise of our beginning
And so we set out calmly into the sky,
Out over sheer space and distant waters
Where other travelers had found harbor;
It was the gothic grandeur, the bright towers,
By which we knew the magnitude of our attempt,
Rushing forward into the expanding light.
The structure of our adventure, the road
We went by, protected us from the view
Beneath us, and it was the monumental
Objects, distant caricatures of themselves,
Which tried to occupy our attention.
Having come so far, we reached the summit:
A surprise, we hadn't been paying attention
To much besides a perception of ourselves
As puny and audacious, caught in a monumental
Undertaking; but now the panoramic view
Of our accomplishment, the end of the road,
Presented itself in the soft, reflected light.
We felt, of course, elevated in our attempt,
Inspired by the reach of the last aspiring tower,
Felt fulfilled in the wish each of us harbors
To journey and return safely off the waters;
And so we were set down out of the sky
According to the prescriptions of our beginning
Into a difficult place, though we weren't particular.

Monument Valley

Maybe the mind works like centuries of erosion,
The runoffs and channels mostly bone-dry and then flooded
With a wall of water out of the desert, itself absorbed
Almost instantly into the cracked ground and leaving
Only a thin layer of fine sludge like a train of thought.
Over time the larger formations appear, personality
And prejudice, a manner of speaking, assuming all sorts
Of fantastic shapes, climbing into the atmosphere
And achieving a shimmering air of grandeur and intent.
Of course, much is washed away that these may remain,
And the landscape of youth is ravaged beneath us.
Whatever is extraneous, or delicate, or less than tenacious
Has less chance than a pack rat in the progress of ages,
Less chance than our own acts and inmost reflections
Stand in a lifetime of vanishing memories.
And we are left with monuments, resembling so much,
To soften the harsh light into shadows and their hues,
To make something like beauty out of such earth.

Via del Bovaro

The bell tower near the courtyard
   Where we spent that year,
Perched at the edge of Perugia,
   Housed tireless engines
Of consumption, insatiable swifts.

The birds wheeled through every instant
   Of the daylight hours,
Darting and diving after what
   We could not see—gnats
Midges, mosquitoes—their piercing cries

Filling the blank sky of summer
   As their motion filled
The foreground of a scene that ran
   Before us off to
Paradise, or at least Assisi.

We paid them little mind, our thoughts
   Given over to
Meals, *moda*, trysts and *tristezza*,
   Words learned new each night,
The terms we found for first attachments—

Gina, Astrid, Antonio,
   Garth, Ann, and others—
Sharing all, even cigarettes,
   We tried to carry
On in the International Style;

Mostly, of course, sheer chance threw us
   Together, as chance
Has since tossed us apart, each one
   Reabsorbed in his
Own particulars and point of view.

The view we shared that year was grand,
    Was breathtaking, but
When I recall the time and place
    (How the mind circles
Beautifully back), what I see there,

Mostly, are the swifts, hungering
    Over Umbria,
The lines they draw in air like lines
    In shadowed mirrors
Where we stare at what we have become.

Where the Blue Begins

In the southern Adriatic, where the blue begins,
We came to rest awhile and play
On sun-drenched islands known as Tremiti,
Where the breeze blows fresh
And pine trees shiver and the salt sea
Washes the likes of you and me,
In the southern Adriatic, in the wind-blown spray.
In the bluest water, just where it begins,
We came to play awhile, came to rest
On rocky shores of barren coves,
As the swells arrived and water splashed
And reflected sunlight jumped and shimmered
Among the cliffs and overhangs and grottoes,
In the Adriatic, where that sort of thing begins.
In the clear blue water that the swells bring by
Out of the sunny Adriatic Sea,
We came to rest and play and bathe ourselves,
As the pine trees swayed on the bluffs above
And wind dispersed the salt sea spray,
In the sunny Adriatic, where a way of life begins.
We came seeking an immersion, to find ourselves
In waters clear enough to fathom
A bottom profoundly blue, to see it seemed
All the way to Greece or any other site
That water washed as well or sun could so ignite,
Came to see ourselves in a world of dreams,
That words might furnish what place implies,
That place might finish what a word begins.
We came seeking clearest water, sunniest sky,
Came, you and I, to see what would be seen
Immersed in waters consummately blue,
In sunlit swells that carried their dark secret,
Tiny hosts known as *meduse*, whose fragile arms
Glanced and stung and burned all day
And raised the blush that blossomed on our skins,

Aggravated by the sun and spray,
By our own attempts to hold each other,
As we swam out of ourselves and were swept away,
In the southern Adriatic, where the blue begins.

The Sound of the Sun

It makes one all right, though you hadn't thought of it,
A sound like the sound of the sky on fire, like Armageddon,
Whistling and crackling, the explosions of sunlight booming
As the huge mass of gas rages into the emptiness around it.
It isn't a sound you are often aware of, though the light speeds
To us in seconds, each dawn leaping easily across a chasm
Of space that swallows the sound of that sphere, but
If you listen closely some morning, when the sun swells
Over the horizon and the world is still and still asleep,
You might hear it, a faint noise so far inside your mind
That it must come from somewhere, from light rushing to darkness,
Energy burning towards entropy, towards a peaceful solution,
Burning brilliantly, spontaneously, in the middle of nowhere,
And you, too, must make a sound that is somewhat like it,
Though that, of course, you have no way of hearing at all.

Christ Pantocrator in San Giorgio dei Greci

I opened my eyes long ago in another city,
Regarding with a dispassionate expression
The business end of a paintbrush.
The first face I saw was wonderful,
As dreamy-eyed as I was unimpressed:
The artist had starved himself for days
Preparing the high dome of my forehead,
The impossible gesture of my right hand.
Since then faces have come and gone,
And the thick smoke of incense has settled
As softly as the veil of memory settles.
I know there are small saints beside me
In poor condition. I forget their names;
The words they spoke I have forgotten.
I know the gold leaf behind me is light,
I feel its bright suffusion of my features;
And the darkness I gaze out upon—
This dim church, the centuries, your face—
That, too, to me is as light, blazing
And impenetrable, divine on the face of it.

E pur si muove

Of course it had been madness even to bring it up,
Sheer madness, like the sighting of sea serpents
Or the discovery of strange lights in the sky;
And plainly it had been worse than madness to insist,
To devote entire treatises and a lifetime to the subject,
A thing of great implication but no immediate use,
A thing that could not be conceived without study,
Without years of training and the aid of instruments,
And especially the delicate instrument of an open mind;
It had been stubbornness, foolishness, you see that now,
And so when the time comes you are ready to acquiesce,
When you have had your say, told the truth one last time,
You are ready to give the matter over and say no more.
When the time comes, you will take back your words,
But not because you fear the consequences of refusal
(Who looks into the night sky and imagines a new order
Has already seen the instruments of torture many times),
Though this is the conclusion your inquisitors will draw
And it is true you are not what is called a brave man;
And not because you are made indifferent in your contempt
(You take their point, agree with it even, that there is
Nothing so dangerous as a new way of seeing the world);
Rather, you accept the conditions lightly, the recantation,
Lightly you accept their offer of a villa with a view,
Because you have grown old and contention makes you weary,
Because you like the idea of raising vines and tomatoes,
And because, whatever you might have said or suffered,
It is in motion still, cutting a great arc through nothingness,
Sweeping through space according to a design so grand
It remains, just as they would have it, a matter of faith,
Because, whether you say yea, whether you say nay,
Nevertheless it moves.

About Planck Time

Once upon a time, way back in the infinitesimal
First fraction of a second attending our creation,
A tiny drop containing all of it, all energy
And all its guises, burst upon the scene,
Exploding out of nothing into everything
Virtually instantaneously, the way our thoughts
Leap eagerly to occupy the abhorrent void.
Once, say ten or twenty billion years ago,
In Planck time, in no time at all, the veil
Available to our perceptions was flung out
Over space at such a rate the mere imagination
Cannot keep up, so rapidly the speed of light
Lags miraculously behind, producing a series
Of incongruities that has led our curiosity,
Like Ariadne's thread, through the dim labyrinth
Of our conclusions to the place of our beginning.
In Planck time, everything that is was spread so thin
That all distance is enormous, between each star,
Between subatomic particles, so that we are composed
Almost entirely of emptiness, so that what separates
This world, bright ball floating in its midnight blue,
From the irrefutable logic of no world at all
Has no more substance than the traveler's dream,
So that nothing can be said for certain except
That sometime, call it Planck time, it will all just
Disappear, a parlor trick, a rabbit back in its hat,
Will all go up in a flash of light, abracadabra,
An idea that isn't being had anymore.

Electrocuting an Elephant

Her handlers, dressed in vests and flannel pants,
   Step forward in the weak winter light
Leading a behemoth among elephants,
Topsy, to another exhibition site;
   Caparisoned with leather bridle,
Six impassive tons of carnival delight
Shambles on among spectators who sidle
   Nervously off, for the brute has killed
At least three men, most recently an idle
Hanger-on at shows, who, given to distilled
   Diversions, fed her a live cigar.
Since become a beast of burden, Topsy thrilled
The crowds in her palmy days, and soon will star
   Once more, in an electrocution,
Which incident, though it someday seem bizarre,
Is now a new idea in execution.

Topsy has been fed an unaccustomed treat,
   A few carrots laced with cyanide,
And copper plates have been fastened to her feet,
Wired to cables running off on either side;
   She stamps two times in irritation,
Then waits, for elephants, having a thick hide,
Know how to be patient. The situation
   Seems dreamlike, till someone throws a switch,
And the huge body shakes for the duration
Of five or six unending seconds, in which
   Smoke rises and Topsy's trunk contracts
And twelve thousand mammoth pounds finally pitch
To earth, as the current breaks and all relax.
   It is a scene shot with shades of gray—
The smoke, the animal, the reported facts—
On a seasonably gray and gloomy day.

Would you care to see any of that again?
        See it as many times as you please,
For an electrician, Thomas Edison,
Has had a bright idea we call the movies,
        And called on for monitory spark,
Has preserved it all in framed transparencies
That are clear as day, for all the day is dark.
        You might be amused on second glance
To note the background—it's an amusement park!—
A site on Coney Island where elephants
        Are being used in the construction,
And where Topsy, through a keeper's negligence,
Got loose, causing some property destruction,
        And so is shown to posterity,
A study in images and conduction,
Sunday, January 4th, 1903.

FROM

Of the Knowledge of Good and Evil

1991

I'm Sorry, Einstein

Newton, forgive me. You found the only way which,
in your age, was just about possible . . .

Forgive me, so you said, with what infinite
    Forbearance, with nostalgia, respect,
Apologizing to the past for the thought
    You wreaked, for the order you had wrecked,
For the world itself, the way that it appeared.

Forgive me, you wrote, chagrined, asking pardon
    As if it were your fault for the weird
Ways things were, the inexplicability
    Of science, for having persevered
Along a new and difficult dimension

Where time assumes a shape and space bends, where light
    And radiation, not to mention
Matter, may be understood as particles,
    And where the act of apprehension
Is distorted by the place where it occurs,

Or just about possibly so, forgive me.
    Ah Einstein, I'm sorry, but it's worse
Than even you imagined, more beautiful
    And strange, and perhaps the universe
Does not exist except as it is believed,

Or exists only as our motion through it.
    Light, we say, and that's what is perceived;
Nothingness, we think, and find it everywhere.
    I'm sorry, Einstein; oh, I am grieved
To say that perhaps we should apologize

For having learned little, gained so little ground,
    So that each man looks into the skies

And stands where Newton stood, Spinoza, Plato,
  Unsure what he sees with his own eyes,
Discovering an unending darkness flecked
  With the fusion of his own intellect.

Keats's Handkerchief

One day you, also, will gaze into Keats's handkerchief
And find, with him, the evidence, ghastly, glistening,
Of your mortality, the crimson drop of arterial blood
Your tubercular cough has deposited in that cloth.
Someday an immense future will simply disappear.
When that day comes, don't think yourself surprised,
Though you seem young, though your ambition, Caesarian,
Alexandrine, has been left grotesquely unfulfilled—
All men are young, everything remains to do, and hope
Is a companion that should always have died hereafter.
And don't pretend ignorance, spare yourself such deceit,
Though cold and adamantine fingers grip your heart
And your breath labor with the weight of what you know—
Having been studious, having made your soul in the vale
Of human possibilities, it is this you have prepared for:
To recognize and record your perception and its passing.
Stare in that woven square and consider the thing at hand.
If you could sever yourself from its fell significance
It might seem even beautiful, the gleaming bead of blood
As rare as gemstone, a ruby of the finest water,
Bright as Betelgeuse in the glittering cloth of night.
Stare awhile, and then put the handkerchief away;
Take up your brother's hand, who lies in pain,
For poor Tom is dying, too.

The Blue Cage

The universe composed itself around a door,
Now that the happy sun and its attendant clouds
Had drifted off in valedictory display.
Walls rose up where open fields had stretched,
And stars pressed down their thin white light;
Beneath his feet, all dead things heaved.
His universe was distance and this door,
Stone gate, grated portal, shuttered aperture,
Great pillars standing at earth's end.
It was the door that made the sky so blue,
The door that gave each instant its tiny tick.
Within were robust wines, garlic, and legumes,
Was water, certainly, catching the last bright rays;
Without, dust in the mouth, a sustenance of wind.
All space was blue bars and this one door,
And he hovered at the threshold, kneeling there
As angels do, to speak the prescribed syllables.
Oh, it was not the habitation he had expected,
The huge expanse that beckoned, unpeopled place,
That other ocean, bodiless and lapping.
But the mind never finds the way it will not pass:
He stood up and walked out of this world.

Waiting for Gloria

for my mother and father

The hurricane of 1938
Happened on this shoreline by surprise,
As what had been a tropical depression
Of only average size
While forming on the Caribbean seas
Expanded with the moisture-laden breeze
Of Florida to grow depressed indeed,
A barometric nightmare gaining speed
Off Hatteras and shifting in its course
By dark, so that it outran all alarms
And fell with unanticipated force
Upon Long Island's cottages and farms,
Leaving less occasion to prepare
Than if the crack of doom had sounded there.
    It almost did, from what old-timers say:
Propelled a hundred forty miles per hour,
Thin air assumes an awe-inspiring power,
And anything that cannot crouch must fly;
Whatever will not weather must give way
When record rainfall tumbles from the sky
To climb above ten inches in one day.
Arriving at high tide,
The storm plowed salt into the countryside,
And crops till then protected from the brine
Were blasted by the spray;
So, in the blink of that cyclonic eye,
The seasons altered in an afternoon,
The fruits of autumn wasting on the vine
Without a hint of frost or harvest moon.
As if by some design,
The hurricane struck hardest at the spot
Where houses flourished and the dunes did not:

The ocean leapt across Westhampton Beach
To raze the shingle summer homes it found,
While residents, left clinging each to each,
Were swept away and for the most part drowned,
Their cries submerged in the unheard of sound
Of wind that whistled by at such a rate
That everything it touched must resonate.
      Within two hours the storm passed overhead,
Bound for New London, Providence, New Hampshire,
And left Long Island sorting out its dead;
It was the sort of murderous event
You read about in the Old Testament,
A wind to shake the earth, and in its wake
Lay ruin unrelieved, as the entire
New England coast was battered at the cost
Of more destruction and of more life lost
Than that reported in Chicago's fire
Or San Francisco's quake.
That hurricane killed seven hundred people
And washed away the Montauk fishing fleet.
It toppled maple and uprooted birch—
Three hundred million trees—and felled the steeple
Beside the old Sag Harbor whaler's church
That faces Union Street.
It put the putrid odor in the air
Of rotting livestock scattered everywhere
And plucked a hatchway from my family's roof
So that the rain-soaked ceilings sagged and fell,
A *coup de grâce* to end the Great Depression.
In thirty-eight, a world was blown to hell
By weather worse than folks had ever had,
And now they say what's coming is as bad.
      "You'd think the human race might learn a lesson,"
My father, standing on a ladder, mutters
At a vista which, from this height, seems
A quilt of tennis courts and swimming pools
Pulled snug around some architect's bad dreams,

"Still building on the beach, the ruddy fools."
My answer is to hand him down the shutters
We're taking from the dormer window frames
To keep the wind from dashing them to bits
In less than no time when the first squall hits;
Time was, he could have done it on his own,
But one old man can't keep a country home
In times like these, and therefore I have come,
Drawn from the city by the storm report,
To cart off trash that might be blown
About and lash the woodpile down, to nail
The barn doors fast and tape the window glass,
To locate lamps and fill the cars with gas
And, foreseeing that the pump will fail,
To run some extra water in the bath,
To lay in food and candles and, in short,
To do what can be done in last resort
When trouble's up and you are in its path.

    In this case trouble has a name, although
Such things didn't fifty years ago:
Gloria, which we think a happy choice,
Instead of something plain or just plain odd,
For what is billed to be a cross between
A freak of nature and the hand of God.
The news puts Gloria just an hour offshore,
And now the ocean's melancholy voice
Is building to a roar,
While small rain driven by the rising gale
Already stings my skin; as thick clouds sail
Through a lowering sky, like landscape seen
In passing from a train, the morning light
Of mid-September turns a shade of green;
Leaves and twigs and blades of grass take wing,
All wildlife vanishes, and no birds sing.

    I take a final shutter from its hooks
And pause, our task complete, to gaze around
Before we go. I'd say my father's right:

Built with slight support on sandy ground,
Those million dollar mansions on the dunes
Seem all but outward bound.
"They'll go like *that*," the old man likes to say,
"Clean out to sea," and from the way it looks,
Today might be the day
In which the clutter grown up with the years
On what had been the countryside of youth
(Houses strewn where he can still see fields,
New-made roads with names that do not mean
A thing to him, who now can best retain
The world that was when he was seventeen)
Wobbles and with one puff disappears,
Dispersed, as much as by the hurricane,
By wishful thinking realized at last,
Just as the present, stormed by memory, yields
To better judgment and becomes the past.

   "Five letters, anyone, for 'mend mistakes'?"
My mother, puzzled by the *Times*, inquires
Of us the instant we are back inside.
Before the fireplace, where she's set her chair,
With pun and pencil at her tongue, she shakes
Her head and smiles when Father offers 'blast,'
Then frowns and writes as I suggest 'erase.'
Given cunning words and cozy fires,
Mother takes her hurricanes in stride
And laughs to hear me say it's all hot air.
"Anything to eat around this place?"
Puts in my father, perfectly content
To see the wind and water do their worst
So long as he has filled his belly first;
And Mother, even as His Hunger speaks,
Has much to recommend,
For knowing that this meal might be the end
Of comfort for some days or even weeks,
She's occupied the hours the menfolk spent
Aloft providing for their wants below,

Gathering a luncheon that will go
From soup to nuts to flutes of Veuve Clicquot:
A choice repast, assembled with such art
It seems like sacrilege to lift a fork.

    A phone pole staggers as I pop the cork—
It only takes us sitting down to eat
To make the world around us fall apart—
Trees sag and split amidst a cloud of leaves,
While power lines lie writhing in the street,
So that just as I propose a toast,
Our electricity gives up the ghost;
Above the beach, a pounding ocean heaves
Up bursts of spray to blossom in the sky
Like fireworks that explode there in July;
We watch a neighbor's home as shingles lift
Off one by one, while underneath our door
The rain leaks in and pools up on the floor.
The rafters creak, the boards begin to shift,
The whole house shudders like a ship at sea,
And even Mother starts to show the strain;
But Father, his disgust replacing glee,
Just stares and grumbles, "not enough debris."

    As shredded vegetation coats each pane
Of glass, the spectacle becomes obscure,
A scene of clouded rage and dim excess;
It looks as if the landscape can't endure
The site of so much self-destructiveness,
But when we think the world won't stand the pace,
The wind drops and the sun reveals its face,
House lights for a hasty intermission
Of fifteen minutes while we're in the eye.
A heavy calm prevails, and then the sky
Boils over once again, the remnant scenery
Reverting to a supplicant position,
Bent beneath the will of winds reversed,
Which force the loosened trunks of listing greenery
To stand straight up and fall the other way.

Yet this act seems less violent than the first,
And knowing how a drama, once begun,
Becomes a bore if it is overdone,
We wonder if we've grown a bit blasé,
Till someone's not-too-educated guess
Surmises now the storm is in recess,
Its forward motion sped to other shores,
The wind that circles back to us is less.
It's still enough to make the chimney scream
And rattle glass and crack a basement beam,
And then it's over, and we step outdoors.

    Surveying the effects from our front lawn,
We might be dreamers waking from the dream,
Amazed to see the sun
Return us all we'd thought to leave behind.
"I hope those weathermen were having fun,"
My father says. "There's not a damned thing gone."
And sure enough, a spindrift gaze will find
That not one beach-house has been undermined;
But if such human elements remain,
With every rooted thing the race is run:
Mother's flower garden lies in tatters,
And this year's bloom is blown. It hardly matters,
Though, for standing in the gentle breeze
That's been imported freshly from the Keys,
You'd say that any loss had been our gain;
You'd say the sky had never been so clear,
The way the storm has scrubbed the atmosphere,
And swear the air had never smelled so good,
Now that the winnowed grass and broken wood
Send up their scent like heavenly refrains,
Like incense, like the desert when it rains,
What perfume would resemble if it could.

    Have you ever seen this earth the day
A hurricane blows by? You feel a great
Peace descend, and life seems sweet, the way
It must have seemed that time in thirty-eight,

In spite of all destruction and decay.
Those passed over best appreciate
What world we have, who know each overcast
Will clear in time, and know this calm can't last.

The 4th of July, and

The sidewalks are wobbling in the god-awful heat,
    Ninety-eight in the shade,
Where there is shade, as New York lies locked under
    Layers of high pressure
That trap the thick atmosphere (ozone, exhaust, smog
    Drifted over from Jersey,
Infernal dampness: "It's not the heat, it's the whatchamacallit,"
    Said a fat girl in the elevator,
Too hot or too humid to get a grip on her clichés),
    Clapping it over your face:
Today, Independence Day, on the verge of moving to the burbs
    (7 rms, 2 bths, occ. negotiable),
I walk to the window (how the black dust seeps in!) and look
    Upon the city I am losing:
Lines for everything, jack-hammers, crime, garbage,
    Rent out the wazoo,
Air pollution, noise pollution, rush-hour traffic, dope,
    Payola, beautiful people,
Bag people, a new disease every day, cyclical poverty,
    Mayor Koch (yech),
Donald Trump (yech, yech), Leona Helmsley (STOP!):
    Why even Sandy McClatchy,
Who, let's face it, is a man at pains to appear urbane,
    When he got back the last time
Said this town seems more and more like Calcutta,
    So why, can you tell me,
After ten years of such dreck should I be sorry to go?
    I mean, should I care?
Because, excuse me, fresh bagels all by themselves
    Can't make up for it all,
Not even from H & H World's Best Bagels, where the sign says
    "You'll be in Heaven—Share Them!!!"
(OK: oh to be standing in the March a.m. with a hot bagel
    In your hand, its firm flesh
Yielding to your fingers and the steam rising into your face . . .

Mmmm, make mine with raisins).
But today, Independence Day, as a huge, hazy, orange sun
    Sets over the Bayonne swamps
Like an industrial disaster, like gas flaring over an oil field,
    Why give a second thought,
Can you tell me please, to the notion of kissing goodbye
    Cabbies who know everything
And got off the boat just last week? of leaving behind
    Cops with that big-city attitude
And that high school education? of bidding a final *adieu*
    To the Eurotrash crowding midtown?
Why is the heart downcast to think I won't be seeing
    The promenade along the Heights
(Alright, I don't go there all that often, but I *could*),
    Where I chatted with Ben Gardner
The third time he got off the ward? We availed ourselves
    Of that view and spoke of how,
Statistically considered, the odds were his mind would now
    Never really be right again.
And what of the old-world roses in back of the Brooklyn Museum?
    If you time your visit right
(The 4th of July is too late, early in June would be better),
    You can take in Albert Bierstadt
And then find Coral Creeper in bloom, pale apricot and smelling
    Sweeter even than oil paint.
Or if that seems too out-of-town (those Japanese tour groups
    Just *love* botanical gardens),
We speeding bedlamites might cross the bridge and drop
    By Chumley's for a drink:
Left over from prohibition, Chumley's is all a bar should be,
    Dark and cool, even in July,
And decorated with book jackets by authors famous in their time.
    Let's have gin gimlets
(Just gin and lime juice, no additives—New York bartenders
    Will try to be original)
And look around the place, at the wood paneling and stone hearth
    And two inconspicuous exits,

Still a handy feature if you see someone you'd rather not.
  Now that we've started
Who wants to stop? Let's do them all, let's hit the White Horse
  Where Hudson St. winds up
(Only please, this once, could we get in and out without quoting
  His Welsh and blottoed self?);
Let's taxi along Park Ave. to the lounge at the Mayfair Regent
  And sit in wing-back chairs
While the girls in Victorian garb bring us exotic rum punches;
  Let's take the tube to Tribeca,
To Puffy's on Varick St. (yes, I know Puffy's is all yuppies now—
  Too close to the exchanges,
And besides, artists can't afford Tribeca anymore—but today
  Everyone's left for the 4th
And we can drink in peace as the trucks coming out of the tunnel
  Rumble past warehouses outside).
Look, let's really celebrate—come on, I'm leaving this town—
  I know an opium den
Not far from the Manhattan Bridge (that engineering embarrassment,
  That rickety hodgepodge,
That architectural macaronic of gothic arches and filigree finials
  And some sort of Brandenburg Gate
Providing triumphal entry to the stoplights along Flatbush Ave.),
  And if we beg at the door
We might just get in, even though we don't speak Chinese
  And have big noses and smell bad.
What do you mean you don't want to? What else is New York for?
  Costly hangovers and cheap ennui,
So come on, and since we're half-drunk and headed in that direction,
  Let's stop at Diamond Lil's,
The joint on Canal where Rick Tilton used to get flat polluted
  As he drank and drew the dancers
(All the models a painter could ask for, right there on the bar,
  And striking *most* unusual poses),
Only—damn!—I forgot, Diamond Lil's is now McDonald's, and that
  Is the trouble with this town:
Just when you get used to it, get to know your way around,

The city you have learned is gone,
Torn down and made over according to someone else's blueprint
    Of how New York should be,
The landscape of your desires replaced by one more up-to-date,
    By something more profitable
(Building New York making politicians so much money they elect
    To repeat the effect regularly),
So that if you go looking for McFeely's, in the Terminal Hotel
    At the west end of 23rd,
Where Dan Halpern and Stephen Spender came in to eat one night
    With a copy of Schuyler's poem
Called "Dining Out with Doug and Frank," which takes place there,
    And started reading it aloud
Without even noticing—dumb bunnies—that sitting right next to them
    Were Doug and Frank in the flesh,
You'll find it's closed, kaput, in renovation, i.e. done for;
    And if you go looking
At the head of MacDougal for the Eighth St. Bookstore,
    Where my poems will never stand
Between Byron and Blake (and right next to Charles Bukowski:
    Sometimes life is pure bathos),
You'll find it's disappeared, vanished like volumes out-of-print,
    Literally gone up in smoke,
And if New York has its bookstores still, still none of them,
    Not Gotham Bookmart
(It's clubby and confuses literature with rock n' roll, but stocks
    Plenty of poetry anyway),
Not Books & Co. (spruce, with a so-so poetry selection unaccountably
    Interspersed with prose),
Not the Phoenix, Gryphon, St. Marks, not Coliseum, not the Strand,
    No none of them approach
That paragon, that platonic ideal, that paradise of bibliophiles,
    Eighth St. Bookstore of my mind!
And that, of course, is the landfill it's all been dragged to,
    The suburb it's all moved into,
The city of my recollection become the province of thought,
    its buildings suddenly transported,

Transformed into an imagined land, a half-visible locale
    Where Kim Rogal and David Kalstone
(Each genial, myopic, bemused) may still be found at parties;
    Where some celluloid *obscurité*
Still shows nightly to the faithful lined up outside the Thalia
    (Inside are popcorn-eating mice
And the feeling of being between decks on a tramp steamer);
    Where those old synagogues
On the lower east side, with their snaky, oriental motifs,
    And those upper west side churches,
With their quasi-military towers and turrets, all still stand
    (Churches are like women for me . . .
Worship seems a bit excessive, but I do like to look at them),
    And the trashy condos
That replaced them are stripped, gutted, dynamited, razed;
    Where the Day Line still plies
Hudson's River, pushing upstream all the way to Poughkeepsie
    To return among green prospects
Past Storm King and the Tappan Zee, past the Palisades
    (That beetling escarpment
In which geologic time is evident as writing on a wall),
    Back to New York, Sin City,
Wick to the wicked and home to eight million aspirations:
    City of unnatural light,
City of squalor and big ambition, O infinitely human city,
    Your every aspect I have
At heart from this day Fourth as the secret that defines me,
    A Central Park of the soul,
Composed of all the beauty and violence that is the past,
    A darkening confine from which
Patens of memory will rise like poems, like the explosions
    That have now begun to burst
Above the Park, above the Battery (when I lived in Brooklyn,
    In a factory in the ghetto,
Holidays would bring fireworks over Manhattan and brisk reports
    Of gunfire throughout Fort Greene),
In radiant showers of red and white and blue, a first-class farewell,

A really super send-off,
The simply dazzling evanescence ("One lollapalooza of a show!"
   "Rip-snorting entertainment!"
"Mesmerizing, jaw-gritting excitement!") that is what I take away
   On July 4th 1988, Independence Day.

The Fairy Tale that Grew Up

In light of the sun setting among gathering clouds,
And considering the countryside had grown gloomy,
With muddy ice collecting in the rutted fields
And stripped trees black as gibbets against the sky,
Considering no steps could be taken that might lead
Back to the verdant memory of your naïve beginning,
The crooked house you happened on wasn't uninviting.
Hard to say at first if it might be inhabited:
No smoke rose from its chimney, though cold bit hard,
And the guttering illumination of its windowpanes
Might have been the last reflection of the day.
But it was candlelight, and the hearth held coals;
Your cries and insistent knock eliciting no answer,
You had forced the flimsy door and walked right in.
A table stood in the obscure room you entered,
And on it lay an open book lit by a single taper.
The house was quiet, and the interior so shadowed,
That though space was small and his chair hard by,
You somehow hadn't seen the stranger till he spoke:
"How old am I?" he asked, and you said he was old,
For his shriveled hands shook, and his beard flowed,
And his faint voice surely had been silent many years.
Dark colors glittered in his robe, and the soft light
Gleamed in the wispy aureole of his white hair.
"Pass me the book," he said, and you did, glancing
At the unknown language there, its cryptic annotation.
He seemed to have no other thought for you, but read,
And in his mouth that indecipherable text became
A glorious history you had heard somewhere before,
Had disremembered and longed for more than you knew,
Of distant origins along the flowered banks of rivers,
Of an inevitable end in loud fire and crevassed earth.
His harshest words seemed strangely sweet, and suddenly
The chamber filled with ghosts, harmonious voices,
Your whole body resonating wildly with that choir.

The sound that issued your ears accepted lovingly,
As you joined that complex canticle and wept for joy;
And then it was gone, and the stranger gone as well.
Those silk sleeves lay disembodied on the floor,
And the old man was dust, an inspiration of the place.
Struck dumb, you stared awhile, searching the empty air;
Then you drew on the robe and drew the book to you.
You sat at last in the old light of an eternal candle,
And in that lambency you thought you finally understood,
Thought each serif of that script had been embellished
Just for you, as you started from the first grand line
And relished every word, attended every implication,
Reading long into the unending night that fell
And waiting for the unknown traveler to arrive.

Quotidian

Once again we rose as the light fell on our faces
And stumbled out into dust and gathering heat.
At a stream's edge we bent to wash the dreams
Out of our eyes and slake the persistent thirst
That dogged us through the desert of our sleep;
But mere water would not cleanse us of illusions,
Could not assuage the caustic emptiness we felt,
And we wandered off as always, a ragged, lethal band.
Across the table land and among blue hills beyond,
We straggled to and fro, searching out the shade,
Seeking a certain landscape, hunting its ample glade,
For surely it lay waiting as it lay hidden in our hearts.
We did not find it, though, that day or any other,
The grove, abundant locus, the munificent locale,
And so we made ourselves content with the area at hand,
Scarring it, blooding it, savaging a world
That promised ease and so much satisfaction
And gave us only this.

Nostalgie de la Boue

They took away the changeable sky, all that bad weather,
Took away the sun rising and climbing, shimmering and setting,
And gave him his favorite color always and a constant temperature,
Seventy-one degrees Fahrenheit, adjusted upward in the case of wind.
They took away the hate and love that had plagued him so,
The appetites that drew him by the nose, the idea of revenge,
Told him he could grow up now, that such concepts were undignified,
Were undeserving of the tremendous thing that was happening now
    on earth.
When the first notes of the overture sounded, the ideal all composers
    had struggled toward,
They instructed him to put those thoughts away, all that homesickness
    and outmoded memory,
All that claptrap and paraphernalia, that obsessive interest in the self.
Because it didn't matter anymore what the wailing sounded like,
Now that the ragweed was resurrected and the positrons were back
    in place;
Now all energies were evenly distributed
Nobody cared any longer about the future or what light might look
    like on the stone;
No one wished to hear the bedtime stories told again,
Now that the final, ecstatic, inhuman celebration had begun.
But there, amidst that indistinguishable blaze,
He missed his own blue sky, its wild suggestion,
Missed the iciest rainfall sweeping from the clouds,
And missed his heartache, too, his hope deferred;
As the triumph of so much perfection was announced,
He wished even for the dark ferries moving slowly through the dawn,
Wanted back those flowered barges gliding silently to nowhere,
Oh, he longed for those black boats most of all.

Loihi

for T. N. Danforth

Three thousand feet beneath a tranquil sea,
A hot spot troubles the Pacific floor,
As lava thrust from earth's convulsive core
Has formed a crater where an isle will be.

That hidden world was lavishly displayed
To divers in a research submarine,
Who drifted on a landscape unforeseen:
Bacteria, in layers like red brocade,

Draped basalt pinnacles and overhangs,
Shimmering in a dense volcanic gas
That took the unaccustomed light like glass.

A monster of the deep, all jaws and fangs,
Lives there; it dies if brought up to our day,
Where waves are now, and palms will someday sway.

FROM

The Fire Fetched Down

1996

An Invitation to Jay Clayton

From the land of football recruiting scandals,
Barbeque and kudzu, creation science,
Military schooling and right-to-work laws,
Country of country

Music, come, old friend, to the land of mud-rooms,
Flu, and acid slush, to decaying factory
Towns and autumn foliage fanfare, pilgrim
Mores and pilgrim

Cooking, please come flying. Fly Continental,
If you must, but travel and take advantage
Of the miser's welcome New England offers:
Taciturn greeting,

Shellfish, maple glop, and a local stab at
Wine. Alas, the syrup and wine aren't always
Easy to distinguish, while conversation
Here and about is

Rather less mercurial than the chowder.
We must count on you, then, to keep the table
Lively. Born and bred in the South, where breeding
Matters and manners

Are a sort of spectator sport, by instinct
You will captivate the assorted neighbors
We invite to witness a rare performance,
Charming them silly

With your deep-fried flattery, served in portions
Just this side of fattening, with your gossip
Balanced on the line that divides piquant from
Legal exposure.

Later, dinner done and the others gone or
Gone to bed, we heroes can strive to stave off
Sleep and reminisce for a while, rewriting
Scenes from our epic

College years together, lamenting classmates
Lost or dead, amazing ourselves to notice
Dreams we formed in youth of devoting life to
Language have somehow

Come to pass, albeit in ways we couldn't
Possibly foresee at the time, arrived as
We now are at homes and careers and family,
Come to this present

Peace, or its simulacrum. Jay what pleasure
Can compare to memories shared upon the
Stroke of midnight? Call it nostalgia, call it
Civilization,

Either way, please visit. It won't be like the
Old days, when the hunger that pounded through our
Veins possessed us, driving us into darkened
Streets toward sunrise.

Paideia

My poems are my children, and I swear
on the graves of my ancestors
I never laid a hand on them,
not even when they exasperated me,
when caring for them left me exhausted
and their cries in the night disturbed my sleep.
I discipline my poems only with hope
of my hard-won approval and the fear
of not being right for this magazine.

My poems are my children, and I have labored
to give them every advantage,
indulging them, up to a point,
and providing the very best education I could.
I let my poems read any book in my library,
even the dirty ones.
I don't worry that they might be privileged.
I worry they might be stupid.

My poems have dared to keep off drugs,
even though they're young
and think they are immortal,
even though, poetry being what it is these days,
the peer pressure to freak out is enormous.
Still, I fret about the company they keep
(audiences these days being what they are);
that's why I implore my poems to be particular,
why I don't mince words
about the facts of life.
My poems are practicing safe sex even as I speak.

Conceived in love and brought into this world
in agony and joy, my poems are my children
and better not call home for cash.
I'm not raising any mama's-boys.

It's the mama's-boy becomes the killer nerd,
and I instruct my poems
never to harm anyone with anything but panache.

Semblances and heirs, my poems
will weep when I am dead and confess
things they couldn't tell me to my face:
how they loved me
but were embarrassed by me,
how once they tried to be
like me with small success,
and how in time
they struggled to be other
than I was and couldn't do that, either.

When I am gone and exist only in my poems,
my line shall celebrate my days,
insisting that my acts were brave as any man's,
that my thoughts were complex as another's,
my loves as desperate, as intense.
Adroit, self-confident, and sly,
my poems are my children.
They know how to lie.

Reisebild

Whoever happens on this rhyme
And works to read it through,
Though it bring to mind another time
I wrote it just for you.

Friend, the brook across the way
Once sounded full of cheer;
But the flowing that I heard one day
Is not the flood I hear.

Outside my door the nesting birds
Were greeting the new dawn;
But the house where I composed these words
Is not where I have gone.

I've found a home by a wider strand
Where no one lacks for food;
I don't pay tax and can't buy land,
And yet my money's good.

In fact finances in this state
Are just as right as rain,
For many men must pay their freight
That one get all the gain.

A richer man was never met,
Though his salary is small,
Who cannot cease to bend and sweat
And never spends at all.

I've seen the savings of his wage
Heaped up upon the beach:
Be it distant land or distant age,
Yet he has coins of each,

Has obols and centesimos
And some with holes, like rings,
Some bearing heads of buffaloes
And some the heads of kings.

The shillings and sestertii
Are tossed there one by one,
Until that pile has grown so high
It's blotted out the sun.

O do they pay when songs are sung
Where you live anymore?
I place these words upon your tongue
To see you to this shore.

Ode on Absent-Mindedness

Remember that lethargic stream
Of unconsciousness, the freedom from all care
Which limits paradise for academe?
     Banks beset with souls
   It drifts in eddies over shoals,
Watering seductive meadows where
   It's always August, where the bees
     Hang ever in the air,
     And blossoms never cease;
   Yet among those candid lilies
     And in eternal peace,
The shades remain concupiscent of life,
     Eager every one
To taste a mouthful of oblivion
And so resume our hodiernal strife,
     Forsaking what they've seen
To walk these meadows where the grass is merely green.

   It is the light that calls them back,
For all the dead are given to desire
   Is earth's extravagance of rays:
   The daybreak and ensuing blaze,
The evening sun, the fabled zodiac,
     Or even feeblest fire
   Lit by a momentary match
That flickers to extinction while we watch;
     And though the dead are said
     To have a sun and stars
Unto themselves, yet theirs are not so beautiful,
Perhaps, or ripe with possibility as ours,
   And Elysium is dull
Without the halo that is moonlight shed
     Upon conjecturing,
     Or reflections bred
By iridescence in an insect wing.

With adumbrations as with gaudy shows,
    Light tempts us to mortality,
        As it still beckons me,
Who sometimes linger through a summer afternoon
To see the dilatory shadows prune
        A blowsy damask rose
        Or pollard a catalpa tree;
And gazing on such evidence, I've come to feel
As if the draught intended for my lips
        At birth had somehow missed the mark,
And now, by otherworldly appeal,
    Must be administered in sips
        And on no given schedule,
So that untidy spots, impenetrably dark,
Spatter reverie with Lethe's macule,
        And nothingness obtrudes
Its pause for thought in awkward interludes.

    And thus, as if by accident,
Some oversight of inattentive gods,
I find myself the alien inhabitant
    Of countries usually at odds,
The realm of fact, the world of shadow play:
        Conversant with the dead
And yet still shifting for my daily bread,
        Subject to migraines,
    Yet absent-minded for all my pains,
I am everywhere a sort of émigré,
        One whom the border guard
        Inevitably detains
To check the transitory residences
    Declared upon my customs card;
And though fully naturalized in neither
State, who cannot live by bread alone, nor ether,
        I know my way in each
    And shan't be too surprised someday,
Bemused again and stumbling in mid-speech,

If I come to my senses
In a familiar land,
The water running from my hand,
Returned at last to all I meant to say.

The Fire Fetched Down

When they knew what he had given them,
This florid colossus with the sunrise in his eyes
And skin the color of perfectly ripened fruit,
Understood what he had done in the name of freedom,
Of self-esteem, their first thought was to give it back,
Who had been happy in their miserable condition,
Had been content each hour to kill or cringe,
Pleased to end their days in the detached mercy
Of stupent sense, the sweet shock that flesh is air to;
When they saw what he intended, this monstrous
Avatar wrapped in conceits of agony, of honor,
Their every instinct (before such brute reflex
Was blunted by the dull weight of the abstract)
Was to spurn the bounty, slay the bearer, to destroy
The visiting light, its unwanted complication.
After all, his differences had not been theirs,
His absurd dispute with the divine, his squabble
About a sacred ox and some celestial secret;
His ambition for their state was nothing they could grasp,
And they wished only to be as they had been, dying
To extinguish the moted mazy rays that floated
Like gleaming locks on his titanic head, to blot out
The subtle moonbeams that shone so as he smiled. . . .
But the fire he brought was beautiful, a jewel
Of countless facets, a spectrum infinitely broad,
An aetherial motion they never tired of looking on;
The flame was gorgeous, and they were human,
And they took that gift, reaching to accept
The ember of ideas, the conflagration of tongues,
And then his name was their name (*Forethought*,
Premonition, how the word had frightened them!),
And his pain became theirs, too,
Chained in the rational abyss and torn
Time and again by cruel and busy claws, raked
By the razor bill of what they could conclude.

The Greenhouse Effect

Funny how all it wants is the slightest shift
In the casual edifice circumambient and the roof
Just caves in—whammo!—leaving everybody blinking
And pointing fingers, although who among us
Hasn't driven a car or sprayed an armpit
Or hewn a tree or burned a buffalo chip,
And if everyone's responsible, of course no one is,
Reason why our earthly tenement remains untended
And the temptation is strong to look elsewhere.
As if there weren't enough on our plate already!
People in high places, people plain everyplace,
And now the sky's three degrees out of whack.
Then how shall we inhabit this gimcrack abattoir?
It's use it or lose it vs. use it and use it up,
And frankly it seems the powers that be are rather
Going to extremes to make an unoriginal point:
Impracticality of breathing, self-defeating nature
Of getting up in the morning, precariousness of, etc.
Pathetic, what it is, the human condition, living
At the beck of a whimsical implacability,
Infesting an accident, the mere fissure between
Crescendos of temperature, blast furnaces in space,
And a -459.6 °F. of the mind. Absolutely pathetic,
And the glaciers weep in their beds, the bergs
Groan calving in the sea, the eastern air
Blushes to behold us, het-up haematotherms.

The Cliché Made Strange

It must never be a public thing, although
The flourish of its inscription decorate the obelisk,
Though its cadences be trumpeted from parapets, yet
Its inmost note may not be heard except
By inmost ear, a murmur, an insinuation, an aside—
Though its practice be bought and sold, its outward act
A commodity and abundant, still its secret smack
May not be savored save on tremulous occasion,
On midnights amidst a pattering of rain,
On mornings when the chill air is its own chapel—
Except two people meet in earnest, its heart may not be known,
Paramours, communicants, their caresses feeling for
The tenuous integument by which its instinct is expressed—
Except renewed, it may not be, as it is
An imminence, a becoming, and yet an origin,
The only past to which we can in confidence return—
A mood, an imposition, an eccentricity,
The same old story never told the same way twice,
In mind contiguous to mind the spirit manifests
And cannot cease to do so for those who still desire
Its reassuring shiver, its comfort and disturbance,
An ache to intimate for naming, this nuzzling, this nothing,
The subtle commonplace, the table-talk of gods,
All that is most human and all that is most odd.

Opus

They cut off hands and composed cantatas;
They gutted their neighbors like fish and released
The shape of spirits from bonds of ebony;
They buried populations in pits, seeking the proper word.
They herded women into shivering lines
And raped and stabbed upon convenience.
They burned anything they found susceptible of flame,
Performing that miracle play, *Apocalypse*, every day.
Undaunted, they swallowed the hearts of enemies.
Unmoved, they confirmed dead men in the true faith.
They killed or were killed and always,
Above the smoking city, the vast lake tinged with blood,
There rose a little tune that seemed its own creation,
A lullaby, an anthem, seductive serenade.
Victims, they could be made to suffer—
It was their stock in trade,
Their competence and true possession, the good
They offered, bargaining with fate—
Victims could be broken, equated with the earth,
Starved to shadows and given to the night, and yet
Survivors could not keep from song,
Or never long, would not leave off their burden,
Brave quaver amid ruins.
Melody attended them like misery, because
The bloodlust was the song,
Its sound another kind of killing,
Because the violence and invention were as stops
Along a scale, and it was all a sort of music,
An instinctive rendering, an exuberant attack,
The one coherence snarled enough to answer
In their case: poor connoisseurs of panic,
Their cornered frenzy held the key, and naturally
They could not be restrained or ever end
That common urge and compromised relation,

The uncaring air which they called art
And by which they excused themselves.

Blue that Believes in Nothing

When the gold light rinsed out of the trees,
Heaping the ground with its residue of sun,
He tried to imagine syllables it wished to say.
Black wood of winter stood against the sky,
A brittle confusion, gaggle of branches,
The snarl at the tips of things,
As he struggled to believe a sere sentence,
In the clatter and click of dry objects,
The patient whispering in the soil.
An obliterating whiteness casually came down,
And he hoped its soft insinuation, flake on flake,
Might speak for him the shibboleth of this world.
But the place he heard never sounded like his own,
Its tongue a dialect he never learned,
Its idiom an alien understanding;
Again and again
The blue that believes in nothing
Pronounced those strange and barbarous words:
Freedom, it said, release, decay.
Leaf and tree and stone.
Earth. Water. Air.

Some Assembly Required

The Aerie

My East End home was homeland to the wind,
A source of steady, inexpensive power
We harnessed with a louvered wheel linch-pinned
To gears atop a galvanized steel tower,
Flatland aerie for a nest of owls.
A child gone forth, at dusk I'd climb a tree
And watch the raptors float hair-raising vowels
To startle prey beneath my canopy. . . .
Since then, the copse is cut, the house is sold,
The vanes have fallen from the unused mill,
And all the birds are flown, but I can still
(Whenever memory's twilight falls on me)
Ascend into that blood-red sky and see
The shadows stir, the waiting wings unfold.

A Poet in the Kitchen

West Fifty-third was still Hell's Kitchen
the summer I first came to town,
Eleventh Avenue was boarded up,
the West Side Drive was falling down;
Jimmy Carter was still President,
though he'd become a running joke;
Abe Beame had recently been Mayor,
and New York City was flat broke.
I, too, was broke, the flat was free,
and so I landed in that place,
a walk-up three-room shotgun which
a gallery used for storage space
and where I could stay as long as I liked,
provided I kept an eye on the art . . .
but truth be told, it was hard to tell
where art might end and garbage start.
The premises hadn't been cleaned in years,
and clarity was not what the art was about—
there was clutter right up to the ceiling,
and I didn't dare throw anything out.
The bowl of cornflakes off in a corner,
the wall stuck here and there with pins,
might be a mural by Dike Blair
or an "installation" of Mel Chin's;
ink spilled across some binder paper,
pencil hatch marks by the phone,
might be a Vollmer, or a Tuttle,
or just a doodle by no one known;
a length of two-by-four was art;
an empty carton was art, too;
so was a hole in the plaster, where
an embalmed cockroach was on view.
There wasn't any inventory
and no way not to be impressed

with the thought that passing judgment
would be trickier than I'd guessed.
The entryway was the room in the back,
where a bathtub clogged the floor,
and a toilet filled an adjacent closet
left unencumbered by a door.
The entrance also served as the kitchen,
with no space, but with a range
on which I cooked whatever fare
I'd scraped together with spare change:
mashed potatoes drowned in ketchup,
kidney beans boiled in the can,
onions, pizza crust, and lettuce
chopped up with Crisco in a pan.
The middle room, which had no windows,
held a mattress, though no bed,
and what I hoped were only scattered
books I took a chance and read.
The room up front looked out on a lot,
and I used to sit for hours and stare
at days of 1979
from a Day-Glo painted chair,
contemplating a state of affairs
that appeared to be falling apart,
acquiring the taste for odd interiors
it takes to dwell in the house of Art.
I see myself then, learning to view
this world with a noncommittal eye:
the Russians are in Afghanistan,
stagflation is at an all-time high;
outside, the Iranian revolution
is in its first chaotic year;
inside, a poet's in the kitchen
washing wontons down with beer.

Nabu-Kudurri-Usur and the Word

Nothing of the sort occurred, of course,
not the evil dreams, not the dementia,
neither bovine diet nor bestial appearance,
hair like feathers, nails like claws of birds;
it hadn't happened that way at all, as any
number of high officials with impeccable credentials
would surely have testified, had they been asked.
When the great king Nabu-Protects-the-Dynasty—
who had driven Pharaoh from the land,
who impressed the might of Marduk upon all nations,
who restored the ziggurats, constructed city walls,
and built the Pensile Paradise for no more
than a woman's delectation—
lay down to end his days,
favored concubines bathed the fevered brow,
musicians played quietly at a distance, and priests
intoned the rituals in reverential whispers.
Costly medicine was brought in from afar,
astronomagi were commanded to hazard an opinion,
and the king—might he live forever!—expired
in the complete possession of majesty, attended
by comely eunuchs and wrapped in rich tradition;
and if it is true that bribed bodyguards
and a perfumed pillow assisted to that end,
that, too, was ancient practice and not undignified,
nothing like the lies contemptible slaves would spread.
But those self-mutilating eaters of insects
who lived in mud huts by stagnant ditches,
who had seen the temple of their god destroyed,
their city walls dissected stone from stone,
their citizens dragged off in chains
by a king whose name they garbled: *Nebuchadnezzar*—
those human trophies of a minor campaign
composed events to their entire satisfaction,
impressing clay with preposterous inventions,

relentlessly recensing their unlikely tales until
they had perfected phrase, reformed the facts,
and then the king abandoned faith with reason,
then the lord of waterways knelt down in the fields
to accept the dew-wet grass into his ox-wide mouth,
brought under the humiliating yoke of madness
by a pitiless investment, by that unconscionable thing,
the right word released upon this feckless world.

The U.S.A. Today

Homespun sangfroid composed of kaffeeklatsch,
The calm was as persistent as crab-grass,
And one witnessed hardly any gnashing of teeth,
The ritual breast-beating and rending of garments
Effectively preempted by trips to the hardware store
And close inspection of box scores in the sports pages,
By annual drives for the American Cancer Society
And endless discussion concerning inconsequential
        variations in the ongoing entertainment of weather.
So the city fathers sent out the fire engines to process,
And an ironclad normality prevailed, though if this
Be courage or stupidity, boredom or despair,
Remained hidden even from themselves,
Good citizens practicing the standard necromancies
And battening on their own ambition,
Who in sunlight ripened a rictal grin
And by night admitted into dreams
The children they had been
To stand whimpering by the side of the bed
While the gold threads were torn out of their scalps,
Their rosy complexions once more drained of blood,
The thin limbs hacked from their hairless bodies
And buried in separate boxes before dawn,
That renewed adults, awaking to the vision
Of an order still to be delivered, might hunger
For the shewbread of astonishment and pick up
The drive-thru punishment of one day's understanding.

Experiments in Creation Science

He went in through the top and extracted information at random:
 names of childhood friends, how to factor equations, dates of
 battle, objects to be bought, words, appointments, promises,
 items for immediate action, food for further thought.
He carved away flesh with a jagged chisel and replaced musculature
 with mush; what was left resembled a boiled chicken left on a
 rack to dry.
He poured gravel into articulations and wound springy step tight.
He dispersed the enticing aura of pheromones and added an acrid
 whiff of fear, a fetor of adrenaline, indelible odors of compound
 distress.
He lengthened distance, blurred detail, reduced sound to faintest
 rumor; the walk along the shore became a marathon on ice.
He contributed ache and heartache, turning bliss to remembrance.
He besieged ambition and injected doubt; each hour arrived to
 portion out defeat.
He increased wisdom, and tears ran; a sigh insinuated itself, creeping
 forward into laughter.
He compressed the whole and bent it.
He draped it on any available support.
He regarded the result and decided to start over.
His spirit moved on the face of the deep, and there was morning,
 there was evening, and that was another day.

For the New Ark

Cockroaches, of course, the professionals,
As well as most varieties of lice,
And indeed insects of every description,
The crawlers, slitherers, drillers, hoppers, and fliers,
The gulpers, siphoners, champers, lappers, and munchers;
A quantity of rodents, and particularly rats,
Their red-rimmed, malevolent eyes glowing
From behind nibbled sacks of grain;
Deer, against odds, and many domesticated ungulates,
Their capacity to provide for others and absorb abuse
Come at this crux to their aid;
No frogs, no turtles, no elephants, and very few fish;
Dizzying numbers of microbes, the mutable;
Pigeons, scavengers par excellence,
And such birds as dispose of much carrion,
But no songbirds, and nothing of startling plumage;
No rhinoceroses, clearly, or pandas, and nothing like a whale;
Surprisingly few lizards, although crocodiles;
No coral;
No marsupials except the opossum,
Yet raccoons, boars, and several bears;
Jellyfish;
Dogs, cats, worms, the more circumspect of arachnids . . .
These the companions fit and unfit for Man,
Who sets out today upon the ocean of hereafter,
Equipped with the vague notion of arrival
And his idea of deity, ark of quaint construction,
To bob upon the deep until
The inundation of hours shall drain away
As his heart's thought shall recede, leaving
The fugue of light, leaping and releaping off of water,
Leaving that general dank giving of the past,
Its bloated scatterings, its layered silt,
And also the cartilaginous invertebrates,
And those parasites salvaged within the vessel of their host.

Spagyric

It got on mountains and they crumbled, the marl washing from their
spines, their rock turned talus slope.
It touched seas and they shrank. Their harbors silted up, their mud
petrified to slate.
It got on deserts and they gained arroyos, meadows and they knew no
grass again.
It got on graves and the epitaphs rinsed clean.
It weighted every movement.
It rode each beam of light.
It got on memories and they warped, approximating negatives of the
pain that had occasioned them.
Faces thrust into it melted, tallow to its eternal flame.
Wood it fingered spalded, checked.
Metal it found rust bit hard.
It laminated cities. Buildings it brushed fell down, glass littering piazzas
while intricate brickwork unzippered.
It got on gods and they were superstition.
It got on facts and they became the name of ignorance. Branches of
science withered, academies were closed.
Words could not evade it. They were deprived of context.
Planets could not avoid it. Wobbling, they cooled.
Its wind reached for the stars, and stars flickered out.
It got on poems. The poems exploded, becoming scraps of misconstruction.
It got on these flinders also, that thus assumed a shape, that settled into
evidence, the difference we see—clunch topography of chert degree.
Its solvent bathes all objects, discovering the density of each.
In its wake lies sheer resistance, the spew of what is stubborn. Wrecked
recalcitrance. This strewn obtuse.

Walking Philosophy

There are worlds, unwieldy, dreadful,
Difficult to grasp, just pick one up
And it grasps you, its grip of iron;

And there are sights, brochure-loads,
Wonders ancient and otherwise, but look
Too close and blur becomes confusion;

People, and they shrink from cultivation,
Beat retreats; facts, and the more you know
Of each the less you'll want to hang

On any, comes time for feet to dangle in the sky
While windswept clouds make blotchy patterns,
Gussy up some valley floor many feet below . . .

Patterns, yes, and the multiples thereof,
But they must come to you, haply
As rays picking up earth's gravitation,

Must find you staring into space, puttering
In the yard, out walking, aimless and amazed.
The unwasted life has not been lived.

The World Put Back Together

To climb a tree and shout up at the sun,
To run for pleasure dancing in a ring,
To offer questions old since time began
Yet new to you—what's that but to be young
And sensitive to that entrancing tune
We all have heard but few remember long?
So poets write at first out of their talent
Who often in an awkward age fall silent.

A child of ten is still a perfect creature,
Sure of its affections, quick to form
New views, being on easy terms with Nature,
That never yet has done it any harm;
But soon, with adolescence for a teacher,
It's put to trade, to watch with mute alarm
The world its parents gave it on a platter
Whirl away and like a dropped toy shatter.

That plaything broken, unearned wisdom once
Undone is weary labor to refashion,
For to be wise, whatever else it means,
Implies a mortal struggle with confusion;
And as a man struck blind must learn the sense
Of touch, now having lost the trick of vision,
Youth must sift the fragments of its soul
And from them try to cobble up the whole.

And I, who have arrived at forty-three,
Am made to face anew this childish task,
To reinvent my world in poetry
By sorting through its pieces dawn to dusk,
While what had seemed an innate fluency
Becomes a quarrel cluttering my desk,
The stammered happiness, the clotted rage . . .
A sought composure, page on crumpled page.

What if the shape I make's mere ornament,
A heap collected out of bits that glitter?
What if its peace is never permanent:
I turn my back, it runs away like water?
Sheer fascination and the effort spent
Can't make a bitter question taste the sweeter;
What of that? The dream this world coheres
Is old as Man and music to my ears.

My Poem Meets Tamerlane

Many things happen in Chester, Connecticut,
but the invasion of Tamerlane is not one of them.
Instead, the streets are plowed and the buses run,
my Mr. Coffee radio-alarm swings into action,
and I'm just wondering if a sense of civic responsibility
isn't the instinct to mediocrity, when another account
of the cosmos gets tossed on my porch, containing
A) nothing whatsoever about my poetry, and B)
such shenanigans that I conclude the notion
of civic responsibility is a thing of the past, until
I notice an item about bloodshed in the Caucasus
(the Congo, the Murex Coast, the Transoxiana),
where vengeance remains the one idea and starvation
sinks its fangs into the blown bellies of children
as it has since Man knoweth not to the contrary
(dust is rising off the steppe, say, in A.D. 1395,
and the far cry of trumpets forecasts extinction;
as my poem is invested by Tamerlane, fear
sweeps its populace as the dawn wind sweeps water),
meaning a passable ennui is not short of perfection,
i.e. if the urge to eminence accomplishes such havoc,
surely we need always all the mediocrity we can get.
Then who am I to complain of disregard
when all history comes to an unmarked grave,
when obscurity lies in ambush as each road's end,
when earth is a mother with a dead thing at her breast?
Who shall record the myriad configurations of pain?
And what is to tell but of hope gone under the ground?
Friend, Tamerlane the Great rides this and every day,
and the corpses stretch to infinity behind him.
They must rot where they fall. And I sing one life,
I find joy and the prospect of peace. Sing not
and my bones have already been scattered.

Apologia

If our ears were not pavilions of desire,
Bright canopies, billows pitched and spread,
Painted sails upon the restless main of thought;
If they were not gardens, damp enclosures thick
With fruit and vivid bloom, not winding palaces,
Not rococo cathedrals and frivolous gazebos
And castles of caprice, eccentric merlons perched
In architectural defiance upon the wildest crag,
Then—O Acting Assistant to an Acting Editor—
We might oblige remark, hark as you would hear.

And if our speech were not another dialect,
Our own rude gutturals, our sympathetic clicks,
The odd stress and persistent superfluous schwa;
If our words weren't cultivations and gibberish
To that communal, quick, quotidian chameleon
That darts and squeaks, vigorous on its twig,
Then—O Interim Director of an Underfunded Series—
We might state your case and say your grace,
Offer up the bread that mumbles on your plate.

And further, if fierce rapidity weren't in the air,
This violent mistral, this manic will to change
That rips the sound out of our mouths and steals
our *sfumature*, a turbulent simoom of difference
Withering pun to explanation, the surreptitious
To blank stare; if the tramontana of mutation
Were not always at our throats, why then—
O Temporary Muck-a-Muck of the Edifice on Paper—
Then we might deal plainly with plain truths,
Simply say what soothes, might seek and suffer
Little clarity, accept the sentence of the meek.

But Muck-a-Muck, our ears are shameless, self-indulged;
Our words remain our intimates and the paraphrase

Of dreams, melodies that echo down enchanted corridors;
And the wind that howls above this house tonight
Sweeps our idea away like leaves torn from the trees.
Who will be left to satisfy but us and what is not?
We testify at other hearings, before a terrible tribunal
Of flimsy things: the model irony of strangers,
The enthused naïfs of day, the unresponsive innocence
Pressed to remove us and be all we have been.

Treppenwitz

As the last reveler descending from the feast
Grips the marble balustrade and hears
(The caress of conversation over now,
The clink of spoon on stemware at an end,
The punch lines told, the healths all drunk,
The few prepared remarks dutifully applauded,
And musicians hired to play old favorites
Gone off to improvise in jazz clubs until dawn)
The evening's facund repartee once more
Wing its way across a crowded room, and as
On entering the unconvivial street below
He knows too late the words one might have said,
So I, the accents echoing in my head
Of departed voices that will not wait
Upon our answer or concern themselves
With our affairs, address my discourse
To the dead and find my thought in theirs
And know that insofar as art is wit
Its wit is of the stairs.

A Year in New England

CHRISTMAS STORM DOWN EAST

Over the Mini-Mart *cum* filling station;
Over the package store that was a bank
Till banks lost interest in the situation;
Over track still racing to outflank
Wetlands no one bothers to reclaim;
Over the collapsed expansion-tank
Beside the empty factory that became
An empty theater; over gentle peaks
In an economy (if that's the name)
Based on tag sales, ammo, and antiques,
Along with bookstores not to be discussed
And the volumes that such silence speaks;
Over a new world asked to readjust,
Snow comes down miraculous as dust.

FIRST LIGHT

No traffic on the road as morning breaks;
No squirrels on the roof; why, even crows,
Those bumptious birds, are quiet when it snows:
Listening in your bed, you feel the flakes
Of calm accumulate within your head
To insulate the world from its alarms,
To stall commuters, mute the call to arms
Of tooth and claw, and let you snooze instead . . .
And then it comes, at first so lost in distance
Its tremble might be nothing but temblor,
But building to a rumble, then a roar,
Till sowing salt and shattering resistance,
Rattling the groggiest enthusiast
Of sleeping in, the plow's huge blade sweeps past.

HOUSEGUEST

In winter, when calamities environ
The coziest of homes—a river frozen
Stiff across its current, temperatures
Of ten below, and earth like sculpted iron—
No known deterrent can prevent a house
From taking in the tenant who prefers
Whatever perfidy his hosts have chosen
To fields off-putting to a mortal mouse.
The steel wool packed in each inviting nook,
The trap demurely set, the poison out . . .
Regardless, one poor boarder, bent by hook
Or crook to prove foundations badly built,
Will come to scamper through the walls like doubt
And even if suppressed will stink like guilt.

MUD SEASON

It's all the ground can do to hold the past
In place. Just scratch the surface anywhere
With tractor tread, the print of boot or paw,
Scattered branches shed by timber freighted
With wet snow and ceaselessly harassed
By wind, and should the soil meet open air
As mud, the objects sticking in its craw
Can't be kept down and are regurgitated:
Plastic and glass, plutonic rock that last
Saw light an Ice Age since, what bone can bear
The paroxysm that is frost and thaw
Intact . . . the man-made and/or carbon-dated
Data someone buried to forget
Dredged up from earth's oozy oubliette.

MILLRACE

Each April's different: this one saw a spate
Of rain increase the run-off from the snow
To make the village millpond overflow
Well-groomed banks and leap an unused gate
Into the race, which had not felt the flood
In fifty years. That's when the mill and wheel,
Back then thought insufficiently genteel,
Were leveled and the stream shut up for good,
Or so it seemed. But flood will out, commotion
Run its course. I watched the water boil
Through undergrowth, sluicing astonished soil
Off toward the deep disturbance of our ocean,
And so subside and next day leave no trace
But mud and some erosion in the race.

A SCRAP OF SKY

The bluebird, famous for the scrap of sky
Borne on his back—an indigo so bright
That just a glimpse of his distinctive flight,
All swoop and flurry, captivates the eye
And makes us smile for having made us start—
Has hope and optimism to the marrow,
Or has at least the pluck to reappear
In fields where he was dispossessed last year;
And there that feathered terrier the sparrow,
Bearing no more than murder in his heart,
Will once more wait to steal the nest and drive
The weaker, more attractive bird away.
So beauty comes each spring and tries to stay,
And so does drab determination thrive.

FLY DOPE

Because a store-bought bugspray meets its match
Faced with backwoods when the blackflies hatch,
You'll want thick clothing soaked in creosote,
Not forgetting netted hat and gloves,
To hold off hungry mandibles that float
Through June in indefatigable droves.
What might it signify that superficies
Be so besieged, if surface form a gauge
Of rudimentary fact? This is the Age
Of Insects—we can't even count their species—
And it's our sense of self that is assailed.
Man's dominion had its place in theory.
Cognition is an evolutionary
Experiment that has already failed.

A DIAGNOSIS

You say your summer limp does not improve,
Joints ache daily and the night sweats linger,
Your stomach heaves if you but lift a finger,
Your head spins at the notion you might move?
Then—since you have cancer at the least,
Probably dengue fever, river blindness—
Beseech a friend to shoot you out of kindness;
Unless, of course, you live in the northeast
United States, in which case you have Lyme
Disease and have a healthy chance to beat
What is a tick-transmitted spirochete
That mingled with your blood in some sublime
Moment indulged with that great Avatar
Whose favored child and chosen prey you are.

CANICULAR

Hard, cicada quaver in crescendo
And sunlight's throb a headache overhead,
To miss the season's earthy innuendo
Apropos the rumpled flower bed;
And difficult, as desiccation stains
The lawn and wrinkles liver-spotted leaves,
To be a spirit ripeness entertains
Or whom a breath of evening air deceives
With memories of how the iris blade
Thrust through mulch as if to reach the stars
And raised a sea-green spar that soon displayed
Blue flag buds wrapped tightly as cigars;
It was their wattles, draped and shriveling,
That hung the crepe upon the rites of spring.

PRAYER UPON DEPARTURE

Absorbed in late September's oblique rays
And soon to be the plaything of thin air,
The Monarch of whatever he surveys
Clasps dalmatic wings as if in prayer,
Instinctively invoking aid, perhaps,
Before migration of two thousand miles.
Meanwhile, a decayed world becomes an apse-
Mosaic, blades and leaves enameled tiles
Placed at ideal angle to the light
And shimmering as wind begins to rise.
Wings stir and pause. The season's cloisonné
Glints. The butterfly seems poised for flight.
We have to love what bears us on our way
Or be unbearable in our own eyes.

Like doe-skin mittens, mottled marigold
And pinned up by the roadside on display,
Trembling hands the silver birches hold
Applaud the dénouement of autumn day;
Like light shed from a Gothic altarpiece,
Gold leaf streaked with scarlet underpaint,
The maples' glory is their own release,
A martyrdom tricked out to tempt a saint;
Like battered bindings of maroon morocco,
Like remnants of antique upholsteries,
Like flutterings of copper birds that flock to
Leave, the brightness falling from the trees
Reminds us that our world is metaphor:
A Golden Age will pass us by once more.

IN AN OLD GARDEN

Some cloudy, colorless November day,
When leaves are down and odd uneven gray
Lines show up where recently a lush
Wall of impenetrable underbrush
Obscured all sign of such impediments
As constitute a fieldstone garden fence,
With autumn over, winter unarrived,
You stumble on whatever has survived
Of old New England farms: the border cairns
That mark an orchard gone to woods; a barn's
Mere outline; perhaps a hollow to surprise
The foot, telling how wells internalize
Themselves; and—look!—one sky-blue cupid's dart
That given time will learn its rime by heart.

THE GIFT

for Spencer Boyd

All night, as we lay sleeping, frozen rain
Has coated our community: the crimson
Maple spread above our eaves, the plane
Tree that adorns our boundary line, the Jimson
Weed and wandering Jew (what's left of such
In such a season, tattered etamines
Discarded near a garden wall or hutch),
And hardy, no, foolhardy evergreens
That can't bear to refuse these dangerous gifts,
And so at dawn are jeweled and glitter-gowned
And greet the extraordinary light that lifts
Both great and small (or all the thaw has found
Unbroken by bequest, unbowed by years)
With rising boughs and bright, persistent tears.

How I Got in the Business

Finding yourself in the olive oil line
    is not like becoming a poet:
mothers don't burst into tears at the news,
    and fathers don't hide behind newsprint,
muttering something about needing now
    to plan for a triple retirement.
Quite the contrary, family desires
    are usually how people get started
(well, of course, but I mean in the trade):
    your uncle, let's say, is a prominent
mafia boss who cornered the oil
    imported from Campobasso,
but who neglected to get his degree
    and so buys your way into Harvard,
where it will be your privilege to see
    the best minds of a generation
sitting in traffic on Memorial Drive,
    befriending the exiled Caribbean
dictators who frequent the Kennedy School
    of Government, and waiting in endless
queues for fancy ice cream in the snow,
    You're there to learn accounting,
how to amortize armor in limousines,
    but one day crossing Plympton,
pausing by chance, you glance in the glass
    of what is an overstuffed closet
known as the Grolier Book Shop and find
    there's no accounting (or even
shame) where poetry's taste is concerned,
    and seduced by such revelation
you yield body and soul to the urge
    to attract the notice of critics,
aching to pass for a poet of parts.
    You've purchased the clothing-as-attitude
needed and wangled permission to take

the celebrity poet seminar,
when—tipped off by the brutes he assigned
    to cover your backside in Cambridge—
suddenly Uncle gets wind of what's up,
    and next thing you know you're shoveling
chickenshit under an olive tree, sent
    for your sins and further instruction
back to the fields of your ancestral home
    in the hardscrabble hills of Trinacria,
there to outgrow poetic conceits
    by gleaning proverbial wisdom
dropped from the mouth of a toothless *paesan*
    (*un uomo, i calzoni di nuovo*
su, non sta in pensiero piu)
    and so to learn something useful,
starting in oil from the terrain up.
    That's one way, a perfectly good way,
not that it's mine, to find yourself
    in the business. And maybe years later,
after you know all that one can
    about guano, why a sack of *pollina*
isn't so cheap as it seems (it's rich
    in nitrogen but dissolves so slowly
you'll be forced to use twice as much
    as you would with what are apparently
more expensive artificial manures);
    long after, perhaps, when smuggling
in second-rate product from Spain
    to pass off as yours no longer
offers mystery, and the chemistry used
    in lowering acidity and altering
color has been fully absorbed and applied;
    when the right combination of bribery,
threat, and persistence (which is what it takes
    to pacify pruners and pickers,
coddle bureaucrats in D.C. and Rome,
    and intimidate the Greek immigrant

owners of pizzerias from Miami to Nome)
   comes naturally to you as breathing;
decades later, when you're adept
   at extracting a profit from the scenery,
coaxing it off of contorted trees
   and persuading it into a bottle,
out of a warehouse, and onto a shelf;
   when deceptive labelling's your art form;
when you could write the definitive book
   on fraudulent government subsidies;
when the remaining hurdle you face
   is finding compliant accountants;
possibly *then* you will come back to verse,
   your object of first affectation,
brought there by boredom and a newspaper ad.
   One evening at home in Jersey,
scanning the *Times* alongside a wife
   inspiring no poetry, you notice
notices for venues of verse in New York,
   among them a cultured gymnasium
sporting the name "The 92nd St. Y"
   and touting a suitably strenuous
schedule of readings, and by gum you go.
   The choice was either television
personalities celebrating a poet's demise
   or a highly professional expatriate
said to be reading in Polish, and you opt
   for English, and at long last afterwards,
seriously snarled on the G. W. Bridge
   (by mistake you took the upper
level and forgot to keep to the left),
   you wonder about personalities,
why they insist in affording a poem
   the histrionics of soap opera.
Exiting the mess, you're left with mixed
   emotions (and right there is poetry's
marketing problem), at once confused

and guilty, because you no longer
like what you thought you loved, because
    the diary entries of others
seem by nature best kept to themselves,
    and as you arrive back in Ridgewood,
you have arrived at contentment, too,
    relieved that you found a vocation
where the restraints to be evaded are clear,
    where mature perspective rarely
asks you to reassess your ideals,
    and where you need never apologize,
caught by a mirror half-way through life,
    to the person you were at age twenty. . . .
That, then, is a typical way into oil,
    although not mine, as I mentioned.
My way, you become a poet first,
    and who could begin to tell you
how such a natural disaster takes place?
    And what makes you think for an instant
mere biography completes the tale?
    Besides, it's hopeless unraveling
all of the strands of that *Bildungsroman*,
    that *Buddenbrooks* thick with collapsing
middle-class circumstance (Thomas Mann
    was right about writing, how it
flourishes in the mulch of bourgeois decay,
    and while the training in hypocrisy
helps—the instinctive grasp of good form
    as something arbitrary by nature—
what's of greater value is the sense
    of nostalgia instilled by declining
fortune, since the author's *sine qua non*
    is memory amplified by wishful
thinking and ready access to books),
    unthreaded labyrinth, backlashed
reel, that steel-belted Gordian knot,
    the tangle of factors hovering

over the page and in each fingertip
    as the oddest kid in the high school
tiptoes down art's primrose path;
    retracing those steps is beyond us,
so we won't bother, aware that the past
    arrives by chance and anyway
poets aren't born, or even made,
    they're stung. It happens you're wading
up to your short hairs in the tropical swamp
    of adolescence, feeling the hormones
frisk, when—ZAP!—you're bit by the bug,
    as fateful to you as Darwin's
contact with the germ of Chagas' disease,
    and you find yourself at that juncture
sentenced for life to evolving dreams,
    a willing host to consuming
fevers the unstung don't know exist,
    become a teen-age ancient
mariner of incomprehensible concern
    and disproportionate project,
all of which is to say that the case
    of the freshman possessed in the bookstore
isn't unusual and might even have worked,
    if only the kid had told Uncle,
cancel the ticket and flat-out forget
    that trip to Palermo, spurning
sight unseen that arena of peaks,
    their impassive audience, wanting
nothing to do with the stingy earth
    behind them, where the olives
straggle across inaccessible slopes
    and the terrible sun of summer
turns the field grass to tinder set
    for the immolation of prospect:
all it takes is lightning to strike,
    and sheets of flame can envelop
whole hectares of ancient estate,

the oily smoke ascending
hour after hour, as wells are low
   in August and no hydrant's handy.
Unmown groves that catch and burn
   are a warning to all, eyesores
visible far and wide, charred
   and smoldering ruins, a wasteland
such as a would-be poet must make
   of competing deliriums, seeing
sooner or later, no matter how fierce
   or loving the family, you have to
pole-axe their hearts, utterly refuse
   to become the adult they imagined,
need to replace their hope with your own,
   and, turning your back on attachments,
lie the young Goethe skating away
   from Mutti towards his *selbstsüchtig*
future, turn into a creature unfit
   for their intentions as for every
other employment, and assuming that you
   have somehow contracted the fever,
too, now what are you going to do?
   You're going to answer to "freelance,"
that's what, working a succession of jobs
   which defy all résumé building:
guarding galleries, delivering food,
   constructing, telemarketing,
standing and also serving (there's
   a waiter in every poet),
sitting babies and houses and pets,
   assisting, flattering, groveling,
actively drifting from this dead end
   to the next, and each day progressing
nowhere, and provided you manage to avoid
   an "entry position" as an escort,
don't complain, because that's the point,
   the best way to wind up a poet

is to resist being anything else,
    which sounds easy but isn't,
no, it's hard to hold out, with hell
    to pay and with opportunity
threatening, but give it a little time,
    and the slough of available drudgery
drains, and you're either a poet or a bum,
    and by then you'll make such distinctions.
Anything you happen to make of yourself
    in the process is optional, though getting
passably versed in verse couldn't hurt:
    you'll find that to spit out a single
poem will entail chewing a lot
    of poems to pieces, a mouthful
yours to bite off, since no one receives
    a foundation breakfast in poetry
these days, when going to graduate school
    is madness and your average professor
sells out of literature to set up in the chic
    arrondissement of critical
theory and its anfractuous, siccative prose.
    Abandoned by high educators,
apt to read up a bit on their own,
    your poets are autodidacts,
always and everywhere and now more
    than ever, their minds irregular
landscapes of panoramic peak
    and appalling abyss, accidents
waiting to happen upon the right word,
    and I have met poets entirely
ignorant of, oh, Foucault who know
    a surprising amount regarding
Byzantine history, or Renaissance art,
    or astronomy, or Mediterranean
agriculture, about olive trees, say,
    the varieties found in an orderly
grove, each with its role, like vines

in Bordeaux: the *Morolino*,
easy to work and giving good oil,
    but never the best; the *Leccino*,
which is resistant to frost but bland
    in flavor; the *Pendolino*,
named for a drooping habit that weeps
    at the wretched stuff it renders,
planted as a matter of course nonetheless
    for the purpose of cross-pollination,
scattered about amid better trees
    instead of the outmoded *Morchiaio*,
which was used in the old days but throws
    an especially heavy sediment;
finally, there's the *Frantoio*, king
    of the slope, producing an exquisite
oil that's the basis of every fine blend,
    yet a torment to grow, maddening
first on account of its fruit, which matures
    at intervals and so must be harvested
several times at considerable cost,
    and second because it is delicate,
dropping its blossoms at the drop of a hint
    if springtime weather turns chilly,
so that come autumn there's nothing to pick,
    and moreover in danger of freezing
down to the ground in winter, an event
    that decimates hillsides in Italy
every few decades, when truncated boles
    come up from the roots like clustered
spindles, shrubbery too young to yield
    a single olive with foliage
areas barely adequate to support
    the extensive subterranean
network that fed the departed limbs.
    Reducing a coppice to a coherent
tree is tricky and can't be rushed,
    and it might take all of twenty

years before one hard frost is repaired,
     the way that winnowing saplings
sprung from poetry's taproot down
     to a few careers of significance
waits on the pruning shears of time,
     the aspirant authors dwindling
gradually, first those who can't stand
     rejection, lacking the rhinoceros
hide required to send off new poems
     to *The New Yorker*, there to settle
under a radiator or behind a desk
     till maintenance comes to the editors'
rescue by sweeping them out with the trash;
     and then those acceptance discourages
(meeting success as a poet is like
     encountering failure at anything
else), those daunted by risible sales,
     a skull-and-crossbones on royalty
statements; and lastly those whom life
     depresses past all prescription,
Zoloft and Paxil and Prozac, and while
     America's an up-to-the-eyebrows
drugged culture, and artists have a right
     to be just as crazy as anybody,
still it seems poems are rarely improved
     by such measures, quite the contrary,
Prozac more often shepherding flocks
     of lines best called Prozaic,
which is why in treating oneself
     for the manic-depressive symptoms
common to poets (to people), I use
     that old-time religion, the mortal
mixture of aspirin, alcohol, and caffeine.
     A deft touch with stimulants has given
wings to many a career, but while
     you're waiting to see if you have it,
don't discount the element of luck,

and nothing's luckier than randomly
reading and thereby becoming enslaved
    to a stylishly accomplished poet,
preferably reassuringly dead.
    The object of your veneration
can't be predicted and appears to choose you,
    but once the selection has happened
you will be able to ape to your poems'
    content (copying the eponymous
primate skill and the best way to learn),
    and as long as your efforts resemble
others, it means they've no self to be like,
    so you mustn't attempt evasive
action, but rather plow straight ahead,
    producing your votive images
lovingly, lavishly, loyally, until
    at last you are disenchanted,
freed mysteriously as once enthralled,
    released yet defined by the experience,
taking identity, strangest gain,
    away, and that reminds me,
not the least important thing
    you'll learn by imitation is never
be too proud or too stupid to steal,
    for that's what the long shelf is there for,
all those metaphors leaked from the pens
    of poets who thought they were seeking
fame, or maybe the meaning of life,
    but instead were merely reserving
room in the seedy motel of your mind,
    and to quote the apposite idiom,
"same difference." All right, you've dreamt
    the dream with no bottom and awakened
into the glare of its broken spell,
    and how to dispose of such acolyte
ardor? At a loss for mastery, you
    have reached a developmental

moment of risk, faced with a choice,
   a quandary, a puzzle like planting
olives, given that seedlings you strive
   to establish in spring must weather
summer's drought to reach the rain,
   while those held back till autumn
have to survive the winter cold
   before their roots have burrowed
deep enough to be safe, and because
   the wrong decision can wither
promise, consider the lay of the land
   when someone proposes to nurture
talent, ponder the brochure you are sure
   to receive, for, Eager Author,
you'll be the target of junk in the mail
   promoting a poetry conference
set in an obligingly picturesque state
   and featuring a pool, dormitory
dining, a library/video lounge,
   and instruction by Real Writers.
Now, if the writers are rarities who impart
   technique or are connected in publishing,
maybe it's worth the money, since skills
   exist to be learned and acquaintance
raises no obstacle to placing a book;
   more likely, though, you'll meet with
fettered rhyme and frittered time,
   a hellish circle of abandoned
hopefuls who teach only to avoid
   starvation; and if so, be generous,
dropping a coin in the cup, and get out
   and instead swim off to the biggest
fishpond available, a metropolis where
   you'll camp in that part of the city
currently settled by artists and stand
   in the corners of parties, pretending
not to be feeling too ill at ease,

until eventually you realize
you are no dumber than everyone else,
    and when the ones standing near you
come to the same conclusion, why that's
    a Movement, a New Generation,
bingo, this is *it*, you've *arrived*,
    your agent is calling to remind you
books you blurb may be your own,
    to mention that fifteen percent of
nothing is nothing, is prose such a crime,
    and say by the way your persona
needs a major makeover, *ciao*.
    Your agent knows the business,
sadly, so now you'll have to decide:
    to self-promote or not bother,
it's a question, if effort and time
    devoted to your reputation
might not better be spent on your poems,
    or if careerism is a separate
craft, the ignoring of which is naïve.
    The quantity of energy writers
waste in their burning rage to emit
    the mandorla of success is a caution;
still, if you feel you must join them, you can.
    To make a splash is simple:
just be impossible. From day one
    of kindergarten to the final
scene on an opera stage, if possessed
    of the tiniest bit of ability,
playing the prima donna is the way
    to get that ability noticed
(lift a leaf from an olive, that asks
    for no end of attention, insisting
bags of fertilizer be hauled up hills
    and requiring semiannual
pruning for optimum yield, once
    in winter to remove damaged

wood and improve overall shape,
   and again in summer to eliminate
excess growth, the suckers that sprout
   at the base of each trunk and siphon
nutrients off, if left untrimmed,
   from fruit in the process of ripening):
take my advice and act like a jerk,
   and your clothes will be mentioned in *Vanity*
Fair, your poems featured in *Vogue*,
   you'll be known as an *enfant terrible*
when not plain called a pain in the ass,
   and then one day you'll stumble
on an anthology fifty years old
   and run your eyes over the echoless
names in the table of contents to see
   that while publicity makes every
difference in who gets published today,
   it makes none at all to the remnant
destined to be read tomorrow, and from
   that weedy Gethsemane of versifiers
runs the Via Dolorosa to your art
   and its improvement, though having
disavowed instruction, ditched
   the poetry conference, rejected
seminars and graduate school, you
   are left to your own devices,
cast away on the rocky coast
   of inner resource, and frankly
but for the ploy of reading this poem,
   your posterity's dead on arrival. . . .
Call it your luck, then, and not just
   my own, that by an unprecedented
piece of prosody, the vestigial urge
   to verse, by the miracle of modern
metrics, I'm in the giving vein
   and the mood to chat, the meter's
running by the ride's on me, so find

a moment's peace and a private
place and feel absolutely free
    to examine this offer at leisure,
weigh each word, consider with care,
    and make my work your workshop.
Now then, five conditions must meet
    and be met in all poems, including
yours: First, it's poetry that shows
    an abandoned love of language,
pleasuring itself with inebriate speech,
    and if you wish to incorporate
words such as *propaedeutic, yark,*
    or *cacozeal* merely to gloppen
readers, why put them in, for verse
    is nothing if not autotelic;
Second, a poem in progress takes pains
    concerning its each enjambment,
otherwise it's no more than prose,
    for lines must be coherent
entities even as stanzas are
    and, as any vessel, shapely;
Third, true poetry must betray
    a metaphysical ambition,
since the art is a religion, and since
    a question chaperoned by answers
doesn't require a second thought,
    much less a second reading;
Fourth, in pursuing its own end,
    a poem must be ambiguous,
which is not the same thing as confused;
    and Fifth, no matter how voluble,
vigorous, or vasty the verse may be,
    a poem must have a conclusion,
not an accident, and enough said.
    And that should get you started,
though as the conditions outlined above
    are necessary, not sufficient,

often your start will be startlingly bad,
  yet do not despair, but remember
Virgil, no less, who is said to have said
  his poems began as inchoate
blobs that had to be licked into shape
  as bear cubs are formed by their mothers,
which illustration, if not the new
  zoology, remains a metaphor
grizzly with unaging intellect when
  it comes to the role of revision,
molder of brightly beslobbered beasts
  and patron saint of poets,
call him San Remedio, invoked
  in the hour of need to polish
erstwhile unreadable verses or put
  them out of their ill-made misery,
mercifully striking what cannot be saved,
  and OK, there you have it,
that's as helpful as I get, and as such
  will have to do and conceivably
might, for wise to the second glance
  that constitutes art's unsettling
gaze, by now you must be prepared—
  ephebe seduced and abandoned,
bit by ambition and stubborn enough
  to persist in ancestral folly—
ready at last for the olive oil trade.
  To tell the truth, you're probably
ready for anything now, who
  have profited little by employment,
labored to acquire no expertise
  beyond an arcane avocation;
lost to the world of sensible work,
  you'll find yourself in pipe dreams
puffed by others, at continual risk
  because you appear to be idle,
staring out windows for much of the day

with a blank, if not empty, expression,
letting the ideas arrive, an act
    which drives your average relative
batty and leads in-laws to despond
    and so suggest a business
venture involving the FDA,
    for God's sake, and multinational
paperwork, and, Reader, I told them yes,
    and oh, about this idleness
issue—a charge so damning and vague,
    like emotional abuse or latent
racism, that poets will tender claims
    for art's industry and banausic
import in hope they not be condemned
    as superfluous and inherently worthless
drones rather than worker bees,
    those fundamentally American
moral insects—I've heard about
    enough, I don't wish to discuss it,
period, but instead hereby propose
    to do so much to alleviate
human misery in the remaining lines
    of this poem that poets forever
after will be unconditionally absolved
    of a thing so shopworn as utility.
Ready? For canker sores (don't laugh,
    I'm serious; look, living
isn't that different from writing: you solve
    the small problems, since big ones
have to resolve themselves), ignore
    the folk remedy of baking
soda, which saliva soon washes away,
    the pH of the mucous membrane
left unchanged, but rather obtain
    a prescription for silver nitrate,
cauterize each little festering wound,
    and rinse with a good disinfectant.

Your tormented mouth will heal
   by morning, and your temporarily
hobbled speech flow freely again.
   For dandruff, don't listen to hairdressers
pushing pricey medicated shampoos.
   The problem in almost all cases
isn't disease but a dry scalp,
   and too much soap is directly
counterproductive. What you want
   to do is remove the squamous
scurf by massaging with some sort of grit
   (the baking soda you purchased
earlier but didn't use is just
   the thing), and every so often
wash and rinse with a product designed
   to maintain follicle moisture.
Lastly, for piles, you'd better forget
   pomades and pads, which rectify
nothing, and instead send out for ice
   (alas, not to mix cocktails:
alcohol only thins the blood
   and further inflates the swollen
blebs, even as aspirin does)
   to attack the problem directly,
sitting in ice water and holding cubes
   against the offending area.
This will require concentration, but life
   asks courage of us at unlikely
moments, and there is little to gain
   in any pursuit that doesn't
come with its share of discomfort; take
   the gathering of olives, for instance,
which is the last harvest of the year,
   occurring in early November,
after the wind has shifted to the north
   and winter rains begin falling;
nearly frozen, the olives are cold

as marble chips, the bearing
branches studded with rough twigs,
    and so the pickers must bandage
fingers and wield forceps to strip
    the fruit, collected by preference
slightly shy of ripe, from limbs
    inclined above the stony
slope but disinclined to yield.
    The men and women bringing
in such crops are indigenous as the trees,
    and of course one's called Maria,
dressed in boots and skirt and scarf;
    today—imagine!—is Maria's
final day among these hills
    in which she's spent her seventy
years, for after the harvest she plans
    to live with relatives in the city;
pausing for coffee and a chunk of bread,
    she regards the valley with oval
eyes as lovely, dark and deep
    as olives, and the long perspective
spread before her, which to her mind
    has never seemed so beautiful,
surely will never look the same
    without her, will be missing
something of its sweetness, although
    the haze remain to soften
outlines of all particulars and the hills
    continue their blue recession,
first the ridge with the olive press,
    then farther off the little
town where Maria's *marito* was born,
    then places she has heard of,
never having been, and then
    the shimmering lines she cannot
name as they dissolve into the sky,
    so lovely that just observing

them is a satisfaction rich
    as the luscious, electric liquid
which is soon to be expressed
    from pomace spread on circular
mats of straw, the pallets stacked
    and squeezed for twenty minutes,
minimum, while unction oozes forth,
    a raw result inducing
tears and green as antifreeze
    at first, but transmuted over
time to achieve its gold-leaf glow,
    composing both the sufficient
means and object of a sort of life—
    of Maria's—the stuff she rations
out upon her daily bread
    (her eyes squinting, her fingers
blistered and aching, after all
    these callused years), the pungent
elegance now on her tongue's tip,
    a nourishment, a custom, an accent,
cultivated residue of time and place,
    this complex and savoring essential.

A Few of Her Secrets

The Serpent's Seed

Walking into the world they were not afraid
at first, though they had every right to be:
they were young and inexperienced—by some
calculations no more than a few hours old—
and it had already been a difficult day.
In spite of interrogation and catastrophe
and a contact with divinity that set the tone
for the fall of Jerusalem and the resurrection
of blood libel and all manner of numinous
hap, they were thinking of other things.
They had recently engaged in intercourse,
and he was curious how long it might take
her to become interested in the act again;
she wondered when she could once more fall
asleep. They had eaten forbidden fruit,
and she was thinking how that lapse
had worked, that she was his equal now
and not subservient to him as he to God;
but this was not what the man was thinking.
He thought she, too, looked capable of sweat.
So in their solitary way, their minds were full,
and they had not yet made a place for fear.
The thing God called death and the angel
had emphasized, brandishing gladiate fire,
remained an abstraction still, and the horns
and talons and tusks and other snakes
they would meet—the *boomslang* set to drop
from trees they stopped beneath for shade;
the *shushupe*, twelve gracile feet and aggressive—
did not occasion any particular concern.
The man thought that was what sticks were for,
the woman that was why she accepted the man.
Not Behemoth, his bones like bars of iron,
not Leviathan, that maketh the deep to boil,
nothing that swam or crawled or flew

disheartened them, though the darkness came,
and an incidental violence gave out its cry.
Who had now the angel's example of flame
and thereby a stratagem, had also the labor
as distraction inherent in God's sentence,
they had not had leisure to recall, and hence
hand in hand on the subjected plain they took
it with them unawares, their fateful freight,
bearing its planted seed as she now carried his,
an afterthought that would flower over time
into mayhem and various standards of beauty,
into mutual distrust and a more-than-feral
cunning: the trepidation born of regret, which
is what the serpent knew and gave to them
and they brought out of Eden to this earth.

A Few of Her Secrets

No one knew her real name, but she appeared to be Greek.
She posed nude for painters, when she could find them.
She could slap hard enough to draw blood.
She slept around.
She was not one of those women who behave like cats, jumping into
    your lap when you sit down to read.
Ignore her, and she ignored you.
Yet she was jealous. She would wound.
She dressed in classical rags, shawls and hobble skirts, the shot-
    silk cloak and snood.
She spoke many languages and was not interested in disguising her
    intelligence.
Incense-laden atmosphere drove her wild. She loved the pagan
    remains of festivals and insisted on visiting cathedrals.
Although she had no compunction about lying, as a character witness
    she was useless: she had substance-abuse problems and no known
    address.
She claimed to be the most attractive woman of Greek extraction in
    the world, but in truth she was not pretty in a conventional way.
    Her beauty was in the beholding.
The objects of her affection seemed unsatisfactory. She gave herself
    to real pigs, neurasthenic little boys, epicene aesthetes.
Faithful only to the dead, she kept private anniversaries, weeping
    quietly in the small hours.
She was generous. She could not be embarrassed or intimidated or
    bought.
She was not to be relied on for anything. She made an inconvenient
    neighbor.
She was always the older woman.
She did not leave notes when she left.

Advisory

for Jim Kehoe

September's lovely in New York, the sky
Returned to baby blue, the breeze now mild
As breath, and if you've anything at all
Important planned, now's when to do it: fall
In love, begin a book, beget a child,
Marry, get religion, learn to fly.

September's stunning, even on so odd
An island as Manhattan, of all places
Least like landscape: climate cannot bungle
This month without a more than urban jungle,
Without an icecap, or those desert spaces
Composed of dust and emptiness and God.

September's drop-dead gorgeous or it's plain
Disaster here, airborne catastrophe,
Some sub-tropical depression, say,
Originating half a world away
And gaining, as it moves across the sea,
The turbine fury of a hurricane.

Still, September's dangerous days are few,
Whirlwinds tracked worldwide. You can assume
Responsible officials will foresee
Such turmoil; you can count on your TV
For early warning. There are those for whom
This hasn't worked, but it should work for you.

I know a man who paused to say goodbye
With care to those he loved one morning, fold
Them in his arms, and just that slight delay
Spared him on a bright September day
When air turned ash, the center could not hold,
The quickly dead fell burning from the sky.

Based on a True Story

No, not equal to, not ever, for all
it couples in public vehicles and crawls
through sewers as through astonishing bars
of light, of music, but rather a bizarre
bazaar of retailed wisdom and aperçu
happily assembled out of what you
will, so that it variously contains
a woman, a bed, wind and rain,
heaven and hell, a mouse's nest,
a winter's midnight dressed
in radiant bolts of shimmer shots,
its construct *ad hoc* on its base yet not
the thing itself, being for better and worse
a derivation, a version and perverse.
Put much in and most is left
over, the sprawled magnitude of evasion deft.
Leave everything out and some trace
inheres in what sparse space
affords. Pare it down, puff
it up, it cannot be pruned or plumped enough
to be coterminous with its occasion, but must extend
elsewhere, more rational and pointed, to an end
and to our eyes
more moving. More shapely. More concise.

The Two Economies

They had breakfast meetings and conference calls and weekly
    brainstorming sessions.
Our brains stormed in private.

They moved into corner offices and were entitled to executive suites.
We had a view of the rooftops of Queens.

They were heavily credentialed. They wore identities around their
    necks and emotions on their sleeves.
We recognized one another as dogs do, by sniffing.

They commuted in vehicles that cost as much as small houses. They
    slumbered in stretch limousines.
We slept in cars too.

They attended recruitment fairs and job seminars and annual sales
    conventions.
We met warily. We were unconventional.

They marketed to target audiences, operating on the basis of focus
    groups and statistically significant samples.
We never knew our audience. We danced in small spotlights, one lap
    at a time.

Messages arrived for them at inconvenient moments, and they were
    obliged to excuse themselves.
We understood.

They built custom homes and bought plots in the best cemeteries.
We were buried in books.

They dreamed of writing novels in gorgeous locales after their
    hangovers wore off.
So did we, and sometimes wrote them.

They were well compensated. Their emoluments were calculated as a
  percentage of return.
We distressed ourselves for a song.

They knew obscenity when they saw it, and they saw it often. They
  knew what they liked and saved the receipt.
We knew solitude. We knew obsession. We knew joy.

My Twentieth Century Europe

As many people know and a few still remember,
for most of the twentieth century the irregular peninsula
referred to as Europe was not a very good place to be.
>*Sometimes a blanket of fire falls out of the sky*
>*Periodically stone comes undone as cathedrals collapse*
>*Now and then every boy in the village is taken off and shot*

Invasion, genocide, revolution, civil war: usual
and unusual versions of Armageddon reigned, relieved
by intervals of social engineering and widespread surveillance.

Europe, of course, is a privileged place, and elsewhere
in what used to be called the developing world,
conditions in the twentieth century were if anything worse.
>*Detached extremities line the banks of fever-afflicted rivers*
>*Migrant skeletons extend starvation over a clay craquelure*
>*Reeducated minds finally open to the twisted logic of vines*

Somehow the English-speaking world was often spared, was lucky,
and my North America has been so fortunate one has to laugh
when inhabitants voice their entirely unexceptional complaints.

To return to Europe, in the twentieth century it was a disaster,
though not a disaster for me, who experienced what remained
of its venerable culture while losing my hangover in sidewalk cafés.
>*I look for a waiter and order an americano at last*
>*I glance at a newspaper and try to think about soccer*
>*I spot an unfamiliar girl and contemplate a flirtation*

Around me, old people with the past in their eyes mourned
departed relatives and extinguished beliefs, but I felt no pity,
being young and unobservant and bound to catch up in time.

The Itinerary

Some had to crawl there, some left on the run, some wandered off in
  the general direction.
Large numbers were scheduled to depart via major airports, where
  conditions remained taxing. Those left behind tried to work
  around the inconvenience.
Trains were old-fashioned, even cliché, but sufficed nonetheless.
Automobiles of every make proved extremely popular.
Some traveled weeping, some singing, some without paying attention.
Some journeyed in the company of multitudes, some were engaged in
  private expeditions.
The precocious were left to their own devices.
Not a few escaped jail.
It was not uncommon for lovers to walk out in the middle of trysts,
  abruptly abandoning significant others to the nuisance of
  cleaning up after.
A great many were wheeled away while occupying beds they did not
  own. The sheets needed changing, the soup on the tray was cold.
There were those who promised to look each other up once they got
  in, at which point they intended finally to get even.
Others vowed to have nothing to do with anyone ever again. Their
  absence was viewed as good riddance.
None quite believed the brochures. No one was happy about his ticket.
  Nobody liked the cost.
It was chaos and every agent's nightmare, but evidently the system
  worked. In retrospect there were no complaints.
They hurried, they hied, they made great haste.
They shuffled, they straggled, they sat right down and were dragged.
They were allowed to draw their own conclusions and did.
The sedentary often set out while in the bathroom.
Each improvisation was at last good enough, any individual enterprise was
  rewarded, and everybody was somehow satisfied in the end.
They arrived, feeling they had flown every step of the way.
They had all the time in the world.

Lonesome Booze Blues

One thing you'll notice about your average opiate
of the masses is that it doesn't appreciate competition
from opium itself, nor from cigarettes and whiskey
and wild women, or any women at all, really, except
the kind of woman guaranteed to make you dream
of someone else, and while this seems counterintuitive,
at least from the point of view of attracting recruits,
such asceticism is age-old and not to be dismissed,
and what is it about starving or wearing barbed wire
or reading all of *Das Kapital* that makes people conceive
they have a leg up on sainthood, an edge on eternity?
After all, if heaven exists to be earned in abject
obeisance to command, gained in barter at the cost
of no deceiving, of no coveting your neighbor's ox
or ass, or his wife's ass for that matter, of no strong
language, no theft, no images even, then tell me
how is the sublime to take place, how will poetry
be possible, how can our obstinate angels believe
Paradise is worth the price of admission?

So do we console ourselves with a misnomer,
amusement our term for retreat. Yet if we swear
off irony, exfoliate the callus that facilitates evasion,
occasions of such avoidance remain, and what
about the significance of suffering, what about
the operation of sympathy in human response?
These are serious matters certainly and the stuff
of major literature, but probably the wrong
questions anyway, not that they don't deserve
answers, of which I invite you to take your pick:
a) We will suffer regardless, so why not make a virtue
    of necessity?
b) Suffering does occupy attention, and humans are
    easily bored.

c) Suffering exists and thus invites excuse, and people
     prefer absurd explanation to no explanation at all.
d) It just be that way, and thinking about it makes it
     feel worse.

If your answer was d), see me after the show.
If you picked any other answer, you are abandoned
to your own ideas and to the words wherewith
to think them, the clothes in which to lay them out.
Still, as minds are many, many are like, and say ours are . . .
what say we hit the bars and hum a few bars together?
Come here, Mama, bring me a can of that lonesome booze.
Everything old gwine be young again someday, or ain't you
     heard the news?

Schlimmbesserung

One thing they could all agree on, it was going to get worse before it
got better. The dealbreaker was whether outright catastrophe
was any cause for celebration.

There were some who sang sweetly while swamp water dripped from
their noses, harmonizing about how compost piles could soon
be put away for good.

There were others who peered out as on a gathering of draft riots,
sequestering their quality time behind a barricade of legal
objections.

Certain ones rebuilt the storied cities, that these might be freshly
destroyed. The radiant avenues looked wide as rivers, the spires
appeared recycled from the architecture of amusement parks.

Certain others made preparations to absquatulate at need, getting
their forged documents in order, sewing the numbers of
anonymous bank accounts into the lining of their carefully
casual clothes.

Some hankered to go upstairs right now dressed in nightshirts and
party hats.

Some preferred to go upstairs with Margery. Others went up with
Kate. Others went up there with the two of them together.

The most secure were most irate. They shouted and shouted down;
they threw buckets of blood; they beat their kids the way it
used to be done in the old days, before that art was lost.

The merely irritable had reached an age at which they were no longer
certain of anything. Their children called them fools to their
faces and disposed of their disposable income.

Some remained staunch individualists and were against socialized
medicine. They visited the sick with satisfaction and held vast
fleets of mobile homes in common.

Some wore negligées to charity balls. They were surprised to learn
their husbands had decided to spend more time with their
families.

Some were too clever by half. Some by perhaps a quarter. Some
solved their problems with home-schooled math, addition by
subtraction.

All sides believed that the others were ahead and that the stakes had
   never been so high. They accused reporters of distorting their
   positions, and about this they were of course right.
All pointed proudly to the proof found in their pudding, but that
   confection was never quite ready to eat. The sticky business of a
   dénouement was rescheduled for the following day.
In the interim, each sought armor in the truth. While the light held,
   the fight was joined, and the ground grew grumous.
Night fell as predicted in the manuals. More evil auguries were
   observed. A ruthless chiseling picked itself up and soldiered on
   into the gloom.

Teaching the Controversy

The police can always exist in a purer form.
Do not mention the unmentionable without crouching.
Do not depilate until told.
The right hand is better, but the left hand has more fun.
The Piercing Hut is available to all, but not all mutilations
    are equal.
Clothing matters.
Some wear underwear for protection, but I'm OK with a hat.
Certain tribes insist on sheaths, others prefer cocks unquivered.
Diet is important, and a low-salt diet is best.
Envy comes early to court.
Many are the lying motherfuckers.
Sex is important, and a low-salt diet is best.
It's three to get ready and four to adore, but numbers are all the
    same to me.
There is an art to violence, yea a season unto disemboweling.
Borrowing isn't stealing until you try it.
Raping women the wrong way is likely to cause bad feeling.
It's my story and meant every word it said.
You don't like it, you can kiss my cow.

What It Takes

It takes so much to make a poem even a small and faithful one
    bucolic quatrain stoic epitaph haiku's reticent gesture
it takes entire planets whole solar systems the vast peculiar cosmos
    of a carefully prepared understanding

Let's admit it poetry is not very efficient the genuine article demands
    all the light one mind can absorb to release such astonishing force
it asks every atom of our being to detonate the private Hiroshima of
    insight the half-life of lingering implication
poetry is destructive yes it has split more than one planet in two and
    yet it yields no more than the energy of which it is composed

Poetry demands a lot and the contents of a poem are not economical either
to describe even a glass of water necessitates several oceans
to observe so much as a hillock a knoll a rise requires an enormous range
    Carpathians the Hindu Kush and surely Shelley scaled many peaks
    getting a grip on Mont Blanc
what endless rivers flowed when Stevens gazed across the fateful one that
    runs past Haddam Meadows
how many soldiers died as Homer cut his hero down in dust

Poetry asks everything
it asks all the poems that have ever been all the people and places things
    and thoughts
poetry is to seek everywhere to find in any object no detail too cunning
    for it no elaboration too grandiose
it appears profligate
it shows itself multitudinous
it looks to overlap infinity or so it seems to the man at his keyboard each
    morning struggling to assemble materials
poetry wants whole worlds

But in fact it's not that easy
there exists just one world really and in it just several poets and in them
    only a very few poems

The Decline of the Western

It was in my early adolescence that the myth
of American masculinity changed, as the inarticulate
essentially justified loner defending Anglo-Saxon
society at the edge of civilization yielded place
to the argot-inflected essentially antinomian member
of an unAnglo-Saxon society bent on corrupting
civilization from within, or at least from New Jersey.
What I mean is, *Shane* gave way to *The Godfather*.
It is tempting to read something into this, though
in general I am suspicious of such undertakings
(the substitution of pop culture for what was once
called high culture being in my view not so much
the mark of democracy as a symptom of despair,
a sign high culture is no longer thought possible),
and I read into it that, when I was a teenager,
my country collectively became a teenager too,
sullenly disillusioned, psychologically bruised,
slouch-shouldered, acne-afflicted, snider than snot.
Reasons for this development, our Awkward Age,
are not far to seek, newly apprised as we all were
of the chasm isolating aspiration from event,
the self-mockery inherent in each good intention,
and maybe it was Viet Nam and Nixon that made
this nation suddenly more cynical than Diogenes,
or maybe it's a phase any political entity born
of high-minded rhetoric and dissembled compromise
inevitably arrives at, but there we were, America
and I, angry and depressed at the same time.
Since then, the two of us have been struggling
to mature in the absence of shared understanding
or accepted codes of conduct, and O my beloved,
beautiful, staggeringly stupid country, what madness
I have waded through with you, what enthusiasms,
enthrallments, what deranged quests for conviction.
There are days I swear we are fated to remain

irremediable juveniles forever, but in time
we may yet achieve a moderate wisdom
(though I recognize our track record in this
regard is not good), may get the knack of masking
disappointment with the deadpan of adult demeanor
and muddle our way to the composure of a middle age
immune to wild schemes and purist extremes,
trading macrobiotic diets and flapdoodle religions
for solving crossword puzzles together and watching
old-time movies when they show up again on TV.
For my part, I still like westerns and prefer them
to mafia flicks, even if most of them are not
very well acted or much like frontier existence
(the clothes just aren't grubby or the women ugly
enough to simulate Dry Gulch convincingly).
I recognize this for sentimentality, but I find
the cinematic slaughter of swarthy Caucasians
posing as Amerindians somehow comforting.
I suppose, however self-serving or genocidal,
what appeals is the faint echo of heroic ideal.
When I was a child, I behaved and I spoke
like what I was, but coming to man's estate
I buried an idea of myself and my best
thoughts in the back yard with the dog.

Coup de Vieux

for Jasmin Trembley

Protected by landscape, its stand of mature
spruce draped in a blur of needles fine
as fabric deflecting both sunshine
and the view, and by the spreading stain
whose slow advance has come to constitute your

degenerative eyesight, only as kept
in mind does the nearby market town
stand beside the inland sea the Rhone
forms at Lac Leman. Two arcs of stone
jetty do not embrace the harbor except

as you picture them; yachts tied up to the quay
like galleys—so we may imagine,
here was a Roman port—at certain
hours present a half-lit illusion
of bustle and cast off lines to the degree

you consent; the dilapidated Château,
hôtel de ville for a rich terrain
and frugal populace, has each quoin
repointed, its face made up again
in plaster and paint, just as you choose to know

of it; and an antique paddle-wheel ferry
declines its scheduled civic mission
of stitching recollected vision
to the steep immediate mountain
on the farther shore, refusing to carry

anyone across, until you are willing
it be done. You think to let it run,
even if you can't abide the *bain*

that will be its object: Evian,
where those with liver complaints and like failing

go to get well. Guests must be taking the cure
there now, attending each other's tone,
drinking their health, complimenting one
another's progress; and yet what can
the progress finally be that one must endure

year after year? On your side of the transport,
one passes time helped by the unseen
staff, fielding calls from what friends remain
and those anxious relations who mean
well and to visit. Given some last resort

is wanted, you elect three efficient rooms
defined on one hand by the curtain
drawn on a prospect that pales at dawn,
on the other by a door within
whence an anodyne arrives when night resumes.

Liturgy

Who comes now to this place?

A child. His sailor-suit is unsoiled, and his smile is as the sunlight
    in which he plays.

I don't know him. Here even the sun is dark, and clothing is not permitted.
    Who is it that has come?

A boy whose chores are done. He has fed the geese and fetched the
    milk and wishes to row upon the pond till supper.

I do not know him. To cross these waters is no pastime, and no meal
    waits. Again, who comes to this place?

A striving lad. There are scraps of Latin in his mouth, and he practices
    striking a ball. He is beautiful, if only when he thinks himself
    unseen.

I tell you I don't know him. Practice is superfluous here. We have plenty
    of beauty and Latin, too, and neither is wanted. Who is it you say
    has come?

A man grown to his vigor. He can swim distances, he can dance into
    the night, he cannot exhaust his strength. See, he requires little
    light to read and takes easily to sleep.

But I don't know him. Here is less light than that, and sleep holds no
    interest. Who comes this way?

A man in the eyes of others. His hands have learned their skill, he has
    a head for facts, he knows his mind and has conceived his aim.

I know no such man. The men I am acquainted with never learn, and
    they are forever aiming at nothing. In any case, no fact obtains
    here or skill avails. Who has come?

A man arrived at wisdom. His shoulder aches always, and even his
    pubic hair is gray. He owns property, and people ask his opinion,
    though they listen as little as ever.

And yet I don't know him. I hear many opinions, and they distinguish
    nobody. Tell me, who comes?

A creature stogged in age. He has abandoned his memories and kept
    only his smile. It is childlike, right to the missing teeth.

Still I don't think I know him. Here age is all one, and teeth are scattered
    liberally. I ask you, who is it that comes now to be buried in this place?

A dwindled image, a shape of sorrow, a figuration of dust. The man
appears as you have always known him.
*Then let him in. Let the image lie down. Let it lose its shape and keep
its peace. As it has been before, so may it be again.*

Life and Death Matters

Well, it's what we have to work with, anyhow,
and hard it is not to feel there must be an answer
when there is so evidently a problem.
I saw the grimace set on my mother's lips,
and I kissed that waxen brow, and what
other scene shall come to me
when my hands fall idle now? Turn
and turn it, the edge grows no easier to grasp,
which is why any twelve-step program
worthy of the name insists you place
final responsibility for the weight of the world
in someone else's hands, preferably God's,
and while for the purpose of Federal funding
theological details are left to individual discretion,
still the pressure is heavy to stop thinking
if you seriously wish to stop drinking,
or gambling, rambling, staying
out late at night, or any of our inventive
resorts to the short-circuit—if it felt good we did it,
if not, we tried something else—so that even
the elaborate ratiocinations of Aquinas at last
boil down to faith, that is, to an abdication,
to junk the whole process and jump,
as if analysis unexercised could ever be content.
It seems the best advice of revealed wisdom
is simply to sit tight and shut up, but you
can tell it to the Marines, tell it to any order,
for how not to be distracted by the pilfered spark
that sputters through our dim wayfaring?
What is this talent that it should be set aside,
a sacrifice to grandeur, be left to wither,
a caduke deodand, vestigial sense,
the one gift that was ours besides tolerance
for pain and the brute instinct to endure?
A small power and a large misunderstanding,

a hope chest made to furnish mansions,
the humble service laid in banquet halls,
the home-made drapes too short, that's what;
and if apprehension be a cottage dower,
predicament vast estate, why then the plot
we're told to tend is too extensive for our tools,
our little pail and shovel and shears, and we
will never get clear of this corrupt garden,
there is no angel to show us the door,
but must wander in amazement till we lie down
in dismay, and does the meantime matter?
It matters, though not in disbelief's suspension.
It matters, it matters, but as a garment does,
a weave to wear, not some web to brush aside,
as the act of seeing matters, not the haze to be
seen through, matters just as thought
itself, now the solvent, now the solute,
never the solution.

New Poems

A Changing of the Guard

End of day, and swallows scythe their arcs,
sweeping through the soft light that declines
as yet to halt the rise and soar and swoop
of headlong flight or interrupt the shriek
emitted by each frenzied widespread beak
angling in its climb and crest and stoop
to seize some fleeting portion of the petaled
world which yields a floating fly. Slant rays
detail the insects in the still unsettled
scene and silhouette in evening haze
the sailing birds trajectory defines,
till suddenly one tumbles in the dark,
lurches, pauses, shifts, and darts, and that
is not now any swallow but a bat.

Brooklyn *Bohème*

"Why do you buy all those drinks for your friends?"
asked the restaurant owner, deducting their tab
from my pay, and I didn't bother to tell him
that for some *La Bohème* is more than theater
and that those drunks in his lounge had kept me
from starving in the lean years we occupied
a decayed factory building in what back then
was a bad part of town. A painter, two poets,
a musician, a fine carpenter, a male model,
plus any number of casual acquaintances
of uncertain description, we dined as we might
on beer and chips and dreams while depressing
our various families and puzzling the neighbors.
"How come you're here like you ain't got a choice?"
asked the lady next door, retired from the Army
to sit on a stoop, and I think we amused her,
even if she was trying to tell us that for some
a home in Fort Greene was not an adventure in art.
Cumberland Hospital, now just a clinic, in those days
operated nearby, and people took us for medical staff,
the only logical explanation for our appearing
often on those streets, and so accepted us, even
if acceptance did not translate into security.
We were robbed on a regular basis, the plates
were stolen from our unreliable Chevy,
and one of us was stabbed outside of a bar,
all of which was educational. We learned
to travel in groups even by day, we added
a police lock and nailed our windows shut
and spent a lot of our time indoors until
a retired Army sniper and active meth addict
moved in to pitch his tent on the floor below
and befriended us, or at least was seen with us,
and we ceased to be troubled. The speed freak
disappeared about the time we all elected

to move on to our several futures, and what
became of him I don't know, but nothing good.
Of the rest, the painter trained to become a chef,
the musician started a hedge fund, the model
transitioned into a gigolo, the carpenter built
a remunerative business installing studies
in Manhattan apartments, one of the poets
abandoned writing to marry a receptionist
who became a writer and abandoned him,
and the other one moved to the suburbs,
where I worked for a while as a sommelier
and tried to repay the friends of my youth,
who fed me and helped feed aspiration
and whose memory nourishes still.

The Old Country

Each of us was a general or a baronet or at the very least a university
professor, and it was hard to get around, no one drove a taxi,
it was sheer hell trying to combat the cobwebs, nobody worked
as a maid.

In the Old Country, we ate for tastefully illumined hours at all the
best restaurants and ran up astronomical debts in stylish
discothèques, and if we paid half or even a quarter when the bill
came due, the proprietors were beside themselves with joy.

In that land of origin, we quenched our thirst with the *pétillance* of
fine champagne. Even our hangovers there were debonair.

We married well in the Old Country, every time, and our soon to be
exasperated exes began as partners in caprice. We broke only
the best china and conducted our thrilling affairs with
impeccable *savoir faire.*

We were chess champions back then. We were research physicians,
polar explorers, dependable aides-de-camp.

Those days, we lived in spacious homes, in family compounds, gated
estates, all our habitation a winding mansion out of dreams.

In that previous place, we wore bespoke clothing cut in the latest
style. Our tailors were magicians.

We drove expensive sports cars, antique Bugattis and limited-edition
Lamborghinis; we had not the faintest idea what it cost to ride
a bus.

In the Old Country we were public figures and the manufacturers of
opinion. We were business magnates, political leaders, the
hands-on owners of influential publications.

Patriots and dauntless, in the Old Country we were tasked with secret
orders, and if our vital missions put us in serious danger, still
our bodyguards were unexcelled.

Time was, we were absurdly beautiful, and the Old Country was beautiful,
too. Its picture-book landscape was as stunning as we, and we were
resplendent in the garb of our earlier flesh.

We were wiser than elephants, braver than lions, more graceful than
birds in flight. We twisted steel with our bare hands and bent
others to our will.

We were dizzy with happiness.

We were disarmed by our delight.

We did not even notice its approach, the Revolution that would drive
us to another land and leave us wakeful in the dawn, suffering
incurable diseases and shot full of useless medications, staring
at the stained ceiling of a seedy motel on the wrong side of a
dull provincial town.

What a Dog Wouldn't Eat

You fell into it like someone falling through a door
and found yourself in a cozy nightmare of spotlights,
naked onstage in a tiny theater where the audience
wore masks and wasn't above slapping you around.

Your performance was subject to criticism from the start,
your size and shape and every breath you took measured
against an impossible ideal that would be the first of many,
the graded assessment gentle at first, isn't he cunning,

only to gain rigor over time, Son, if you don't shoot straight
in light this good you won't get a rifle in this man's army,
and Honey, if you can't see Mama all night long you can't
see Mama at all, until the day when none of it matters,

the trophy heads, certificates, all the stuff stuck to the wall,
as after minutes of strobe-lit frenzy, silence begins to yawn.
Herding you towards the exit, suddenly no one gives a shit
about your college boards or your frequent-flier miles.

Somehow the audience has shrunk, dwindled right on down
to one, and now it's blame nobody, expect nothing, want
to know who's responsible try looking in the mirror.
It's supposed to concentrate the mind, a hanging,

circle up the synapses, and maybe it's so in the movies,
but here at the edge of Albania nothing makes sense
for long, and you'll just have to accept the absurd
explanation, or even the lack thereof, have to eat

whatever it is they are serving as the national cuisine:
eleven varieties of locust, plus the occasional cricket.
Well, it beats starving. Yes, Ma'am, I'll take more. No, Sir,
I didn't say a thing. Must've been the guy behind me.

Cattywumpus, Arfybarsed, Whopperjawed

Like starlight that sneaks up askew and is caught
in the corner of an eye or not at all, it seems the really
important stuff in life, the dense material on which
we will be tested, can never be viewed in focus or faced
head-on, but exists as mist burning off a glassy bay
rich in reflection or as disturbed dreams shy of recall,
so that if insight arrives, it does so in squibs, and if
we make it up, the resulting warren of hypotheses
is at best unfinished space, no place we can stay.
Worse, you'll discover the more you try to think
about things, the farther you are from an answer,
and speaking of starlight, I heard an astrophysicist
(look, whatever you want to say about physicists,
you figure they think) explain how the universe
is composed of at least fifty percent "antimatter,"
which no one can touch, and ninety-five percent
"dark energy," which no one can see, and of course
the numbers don't add up for me either, but
the point, the pith, the take-home pay
is whoever pulls a lifetime of all-nighters to reach
that conclusion *bleibt ein Narr sein Lebenlang,*
a story so vast and shapeless being no narrative at all,
and hey, why bother, let's go have pig sex and a beer.
Cattywumpus, arfybarsed, whopperjawed,
it's an impossible construct, the cosmos given us
to observe in the fun-house mirror of our perception,
and we're just kids at the carnival, our faces smeared
with spun sugar and wild excitement, alive and happy
till we hit exhaustion and break down into tears.
Time was when poets set their heroes in the sky
(who are we to laugh at such audacious *épopée?*),
and still the rays rush in, as if to ask our assistance,
urging us to make of them what we will, to invent
a contemporary shape for the illumination granted:
today's truth, ravishing still and forever unearned.

Best Case Scenario

Your conscience shuts up and there is enough leg room.
The house red is Hermitage La Chapelle.
You look good in a bathing suit.

Wallace Stevens has won the Nobel Prize.
There is almost peace in the Middle East.
You finish *The Faerie Queene.*

Hybridized tomatoes die off.
Two-stroke engines are dead.
Lorraine Hunt Lieberson lives.

All book designers apologize.
A. R. Ammons has won the Nobel Prize.
Eleanor Taylor will send you another letter.

The cook speaks Italian.
Your software is permanently updated.
Birdsong begins at noon.

Zbigniew Herbert has won a free trip to Paris.
Insects all grow tired and quit.
You win the Nobel and give it to Zbigniew.

You get enough sleep.
You build enough bookshelves.
Yale University has raised nearly enough money.

Love proves the basis of a benevolent providence and constitutes
    the purpose of human existence and offers permanent
    consolation.
The angels wear lingerie and high heels.
You can bring your dog.

In Our Obnoxious Youth

we wore silly clothing: top hats paired with bolo ties,
pajama pants with golf spikes and swallow-tail coats.
We did messy chores wearing three-piece suits
and attended family funerals clad in dungarees.
We read above grade level and were eager to show off:
experimental novels protruded from our pockets,
and our sulky responses were chock-full of quotation.
Our behavior was designed to offend and did.
Parents worried if their children were seen with us.
Their daughters grimaced to hear our names.
We ate whatever food might most annoy
and abandoned our ostentatious diets
(heirloom-variety tofu, locally sourced seaweed)
only when such meals became fashionable.
The poetry we pretended to like had neither rhyme
nor any other coherence, and the recordings
we insisted on playing drove others from the room.
It took us a long time to grow up.
At twenty we showed little promise,
at thirty we had nothing like prospects,
at forty we still lived on the poor side of town.
We gained the contempt of the gainfully employed
and drew the attention of many authorities.
Police stopped the vehicles in which we traveled
to conduct random inspections and check I.D.
Shopkeepers presumed we were shoplifters.
Ministers believed we were past their saving.
Often beggars and occasionally thieves,
yet rarely tinkers or tailors and almost never
bankers or lawyers or real-estate brokers,
we were improvident and grist to no one's mill.
Good for nothing, up to no good, of small
comfort to anyone, least of all ourselves,
in our obnoxious youth we sought the opprobrium
with which we met and invited the alarm we occasioned.

Absurdly arrogant, we were sure of ourselves
and not nearly so intelligent as we imagined.
What we thought we knew we owed to others
(though we knew enough to exploit that inheritance),
and there was much we never learned.
We were cagy, dogged, unscrupulous,
give us that. We were incorrigible illusionists,
persistent prestidigitators, alchemists all our days.
Tragedy became attractive in our telling, and sorrow
seeded in our hearts flourished and grew tall.
Sustained by yearning, we survived.
When the horizon closed in and the roof collapsed,
we climbed out of our time and place
and set our stunning escape to music.

Karaoke Mad Scene

Look, I've been to upstate New York,
and I've been to the Takla Makan, and once
you try on the alternatives, even
North Tonawanda doesn't seem all that bad.
It's true the sleet will roar in sideways
out of Canada and the snows lie ocean deep,
but that's just on the outside, usually, whereas
hunkered down at the Holiday, it's insulated
lingerie and name-brand union suits,
it's improvised festivity, prescription sex
and gourmet offal, and I'll cry if I want to.
Fact is, it doesn't matter to most of us
how sloppy the hysteria gets, so long
as the insecurity provides entertainment
and the buffet doesn't run out of pot-stickers.
The party's on until it isn't, and what is not
to like, seeing as the biblical disaster next door
brings in cash and the chicken wings are cheap.
Here at the end of Lake Erie, let's not bitch
about consequence on a given Saturday night—
that's what a future is for—nor hanker after
victory, dream of consolation compliments:
the process mortifies all participants equally.
You finish your bucket of beer and wake up
on stage on the outskirts of Buffalo,
a jury of your peers blearily peering in,
and all you can hope is you've had enough
euphoria to embarrass yourself with aplomb.
Some will sing when the time comes,
some just foam at the mouth, and the rest
will be forced to get by on dumb pluck.
Out on Niagara Boulevard, circumstance
has been plowed to the curb. Within, Karaoke
Night is getting underway all over again,

and the flute music selected for you at random
warbles up the scale as lights begin to dim.
A foregone frenzy struggles to stay tuned.

How the Forest Was Disenchanted

The tent was just here, and the elephants also,
but Toby Tyler has misplaced the popcorn
and can't figure out where his horse got to.
Mowgli isn't afraid of fire, or of the village
elders either, yet the wild beasts have ceased
to speak to him, the wind has nothing to say.
Tom doesn't know what to do with his time:
school's out for good now, and Becky's kids
all sided with her in the divorce, and even
if he's buying, the barflies couldn't care less.

So much promise, such untapped potential,
and not one grew up to lead a productive life
or take responsibility for his own actions—
not Balfour, mingy too in his inherited shambles,
not the Swiss family, cramped in a condo in Queens,
not Friday, his tropical time-share in receivership.
Suffering the persistent symptoms of lingering
maladies, treating self-diagnosed complications
with alternative medicine, none of them gets any
exercise—they're uniformly in terrible shape.

They come to see me sometimes, when the money
runs out and the aroma therapy isn't working,
and I listen awhile to their sad complaints.
The Princess of Mars wants a tummy tuck.
Brer Rabbit really is too big for his britches.
Heidi has low self-esteem. Pooh has a sex addiction.
I listen a bit and pat their heads and push them
outside to play. I send them off to an abandoned lot.
You'll find them there, by the tracks, kicking a can
over broken glass in the company of a mongoose,
a profane parrot, and a big fierce faithful dog.

Marriage and Malaria

There was one I wanted to marry, and lucky
for me I didn't: we would have disappointed
each other at best and at the probable worst
would have paid a boatload in legal fees.
There were others, two or three, who thought
they wanted to marry me, and lucky for them
they didn't: hitch yourself to a star, or anyway
a stargazer, and you're in for a bumpy ride.
At the time, of course, none of them saw
things that way, and I couldn't have explained
if I tried, couldn't even now, what it was
that trembled in me, that burned like malaria
as I sloughed new friends like old skin and left
lovers scattered like chaff on a threshing floor.
Whatever it is, it comes at a cost, and you'll pay
plenty, even without the lawyers, and watch
civilians suffer collateral damage. When I did
marry (to a lover and friend) and fathered a child,
I asked Doug Crase how a poet should handle
domestic arrangements, and he told me: "What
you have to do is clear, you have to be a bastard
to anyone involved—but you don't want to do that."
One doesn't want to. I didn't behave so badly
as some (no one drowned herself in my wake),
though possibly as a result the art I fashioned
could have been better. Good or bad, it's no excuse,
and if apology doesn't equal repair, still I guess
I'd apologize to them all if given the chance.
Good or bad, there's a cost, and the burning—
fainter now, on some days no more than a flush—
never dies completely or leaves you entirely alone,
but flickers on in its deep recess, smoldering yet,
banked always somewhere, ashy and menacing ember.

Negative Space

Philip Larkin was middle aged at birth
and came into his post-imperial world
dressed in spectacles and quiet clothing.
Proud of being nasty, he produced art
drunk or sober in little poems distilled
from a homemade mash of equal parts
envy, bile, self-pity, and self-loathing.
Some were quite well done, for what it's worth.

Myself, I never liked it much, the verse.
Put beside the undeniable glories
of English poetry, the reaching wild
cosmology of Blake, the tender yet
unblinking gaze of Keats, the squalid stories
Larkin tells appeared inadequate
if not decayed, clotted trifles that spoiled.
The letters he sent are evidently worse.

Now I begin to wonder if he hasn't
been waiting up ahead. Come in my turn
to the inglorious reduced reality
of middle age and waking late at night
to take a piss and read awhile, I learn
the use of poets who appreciate
negative space, not capability,
not writing what life was, but what it wasn't.

The New Normal

costs less and is even smaller
and turns out in the end to cost more.
The new normal is desperate to be watched
and would really like to be your friend and has
detailed suggestions regarding your behavior.
The new one insists on a new word,
which you should have changed already.
The new one is aware of where you go
and knows if you're naughty or nice.
It is faster and smarter and user-friendly
and invades privacy the way Genghis Khan did Asia.
It archives the photos, it owns the names, it tracks
the current status of long-lost one-night-stands.
The new one uses more energy and consequently kills
creatures you never heard of in places you've never been.
It just made your life easier.
It just accessed your account.
It just stopped working again.
The new normal arrives with a one-time-only offer
and simple-to-download confusion and a warning
in almost English about possible side-effects.
Eyeballs like fried eggs.
Night sweats like sheep-dip.
Early onset self-disgust.
This normal knows where its bodies
are buried but would rather not talk about that.
(They're in China and Pakistan and Oklahoma,
in the *triangolo della morte* near Naples,
in Ghana and Viet Nam and virtually anywhere
once agricultural and now underemployed.)
This one is happy for you to go viral
and can come with a virus itself.
This one has a dark side, too, which you
had better ignore, its siren beck
of invitation best dragged away and trashed.

The new normal has many attachments.
It retails tall stories and tells many jokes
and does not know the meaning of humor.
Tireless, agile, exacting, stupid,
wide as the sky, deep as the ocean,
shallow as one coat of paint,
the new normal has a life of its own.
It will be there when you have logged out.

Sonnenuntergangstraurigkeit

Pausing to think about the average extant antenna,
how much it has retracted, how far it is willing to go
in its headlong shrivel from every present reception
or the restorative nostalgia once implicated in echo,
counting heads and multiplying by two to see how few
are the ears conservatory-trained in enchantment,
one becomes newly solicitous regarding the future,
its grudging yet vast capacity for offering attention.

Is the chair comfortable? Is the light alright? Could
I fix you something to drink? Anything I can do to help,
anything at all, just say so. Oh, and sorry about the words,
obsolete of course and recherché even in their day,
I admit, but I was in love, aren't we all, and anyway
try them out awhile and suddenly they may seem
to be the ones you know but dressed in other clothes,
old friends grown fluent in a charming foreign tongue.

And sorry about the sadness, too, it couldn't be helped,
the melancholy welling up like groundwater seeping
into your basement, the tears at the heart of things,
etc. It wasn't as simple as mere self-pity, I swear
(though that's a thing we were good at), but was more
the rueful sweetness found in last drops of wine,
the pretty distress of crimson skies, a sigh at sunset
as our culture lit itself on fire and slid over the horizon.

Diet Tips of the Porn Stars

You don't want to know, or if you do you'll feel
cheap about it later. Truth is, they throw
up a lot, and how sexy is that? Besides, why
what they do in their off hours should stimulate
anyone's curiosity is mysterious, since apart
from the improbable acts we know them by
they much resemble us. Like housewives
or high school wrestlers, these kids from Kansas
are forever seeking to defy morphology,
trying to lose weight while maintaining
unlikely levels of peak performance, *schtupping*
on empty, exerting themselves in starvation
like ballerinas, only with implants, and if
they seem superficial souls, if appearing
buff is a job requirement and looking dumb
is essential to the attraction, if the home-town
exterior they started with was simply not enough,
remember it's the audience that defines the art
form always, desire eliciting its object, interest
its occasion, and thus these artificial, not
to say surreal, shapes embody expectations
each viewer comes equipped with, the inflated
anatomy like the silly story line, a reliable cliché
fulfilled sufficiently to reassure (and altered
just enough to hold) someone's dim attention.

But about the diet, I don't care what you
think, it's not what you think. If you are
thinking filthy, know that no kind of star
lives by bodily effluents alone, any more
than on manna or ambrosia or honeydew.
If you are thinking fancy, well these poor
actors are too miserably paid to hire real
nutritionists or pony up for shots of vitamin B.

Instead, they are typically forced to improvise,
doing what they do on polyester upholstery
after snacking on leftovers of a marginal meal.
Truth is, they can get by on almost anything.
Soggy potato chips. Discarded strands of string
cheese. Old nachos. Yesterday's cold french fries.

Pervigilium

Finding someone stuffed the bed with thoughts
(some ancestor, perhaps, or child, or spouse),
that quilt could not contain or dream dispel,
I rose to wander through the drafty house
like drifting mist and wonder if I'd caught
a chill, till putting on another layer
while turning up the heat, I chose a chair
and took a volume down to read a spell.
Soon, insomnia seemed no great matter
compared to conscience-stricken vigils kept
by devout authors fiendishly adept
at qualms far from my own. Then, as a patter
of rain arrived with dawn's impartial light,
I fell asleep, and day brought back my night.

Penicillin and the Anthropocene Apocalypse

Penicillin was discovered in a moldy petri dish
in 1928 and by the '40s was called a miracle drug
and by the '50s had become both widely available
and cheap, which is to say that penicillin arrived
in time for me, who without it would have died
a child on more than one occasion, but didn't
and grew to see the things around me die instead.
My first cat was struck by a car on Daniels Lane,
I was five. My father's mother died when I was six,
my mother's three years later, then a godmother,
an uncle, a favorite aunt, and then the floodgates
opened as generations passed away in the way
of the world, my parents, my in-laws, eventually
my brother, and meanwhile the world around me
seemed to abide, but let's not be fooled by that.
The fireflies I loved to trap on summer evenings
and leave in jars to flash till dawn like captured
starlight at some point blinked their final blink,
I haven't seen one in ages. The phosphorescent
algae that set waves on fire off Gibson's Beach
and dressed a midnight skinny-dip with ribbons
of liquid flame have dwindled through the years
and all but disappeared, and now every dip is dim.
The glacier at Entrèves, in whose chilly atmosphere
I hiked from bar to bar to sip aperitifs, retreated
up its valley at modern glacial speed, one decade,
and with it went the primulas and alpine edelweiss.
The birds and bees and dogwood trees, the frogs,
the reefs, the plentiful fish nonetheless fished out,
creatures great and small are rushing to extinction
in the Anthropocene apocalypse that will surely be
our signature, our sign, the fossil record of our era.
A generation arrives, a generation departs, and you
can't take it with you, but ours has certainly tried,

and what world will we bequeath to our posterity
as suns rise, winds whirl, and rivers run to the sea?
What is ours to leave but guilt and mute regret,
whose scientific progress proved a devil's bargain,
whose each advance was a next step into oblivion?
Annihilators, executioners, poisoners, assassins,
our time on earth has been the most destructive ever,
albeit the only one possible for me, who in any other
would have felt no need for mourning or remorse
but might have remained an innocent always:
young, blameless, and dead.

Den Tid, den Sorg

for Diderik Finne

The Norsemen, who made their mark in what we call
the Middle Ages and traveled by sun and stars
from Syria to the Arctic circle, Newfoundland
to the Caspian Sea, understood their environment
using an ax and were connoisseurs of distress.
Unto each time its sorrow, all sorrow in good time,
said the Norsemen, who were not much interested
in merciful gods and had no faith in peace.
Exploring, plundering, destroying, even trading,
they exported walrus tusks, furs, timber, slaves,
and violence from a place no one ever invaded
except swift death, that followed even there.
—Fjolnir went to urinate and drowned in a vat of mead.
—Sveigdir chased magic dwarfs and vanished into a boulder.
—Vanlandi slept poorly and was trampled to death by nightmares.
—Dag fought over a sparrow and died impaled by a pitchfork.
One sorrow at a time, each sorrow to its time,
the Norsemen said, who left their battered bodies
buried in the boat-shaped graves of bleak churchyards
or cached under heaps of earth beside the distant rivers
or strewn on the ocean floor under miles of open water.
Never fully defeated, they gave up roving at last when
guns replaced spears and nation states grew strong.
Some went home to eat barley porridge on stony farms.
Some returned to the dangerous profession of fishing
and lived on seasonal migrations of herring and salmon.
Some just stayed in the last place they came to,
settling down and blending with the local population.
There they died, and there the children became us,
who sell our slaves more surreptitiously than they did
and are rarely good with a sword. Slowly their world
gave way to more civilized versions of conflict, wherein
they would likely have found small joy, unimpressed

as they were by cant or ideological concerns. *Den Tid, den Sorg,* said the Norsemen. They did not exterminate except when stealing. They did not pretend to improve. They did not shrink from the misery at hand.
No sorrow but in time, sorrow enough by and by.

When Pigs Fly

Never, though more than you might think.
Pigs were seen over Tuscany in the summer
of 2014, when it rained every day of July.
That year the *prosciutto* was not up to par.
In the autumn of 2008, and also in 2012, a man
of color was elected President, and squadrons
of pigs flew maneuvers over Washington, D.C.
Large portions of the Indian Ocean leaped
on dry land in December of 2004: a populace
drowned, but the pigs flapped safely away.
Pigs navigated the thin air above Mont Blanc
starting about 1995, whereupon the glacier
above Entrèves began its headlong retreat.
The Soviet Union dissolved in slow motion
during 1989, while drunk pigs looped the loop.

When it beggars belief, when even a child
knows not to harbor faint hope, some wonders
occur only by the miracle of pigs taking wing,
and they don't, but have in a blue moon for me.
Pigs salted the rainclouds of New Haven in 1985
as my first book was accepted for publication.
The pigs were thick in the breathtaking sky
of Wyoming in 1971, when I lost my grip
on Devil's Tower but found the end of my rope.
Hovering above my unmade bed, airborne pigs
were less amazed than I the first time a woman
settled on me for sex. August something, 1969.
In 1955, at the age of two, I reached a hospital
with a burst appendix and lived to witness pigs
sail through the wards wearing surgical masks.

When it wants magic, when a ranch staked
against its occasion would be too small a bet,
flat-out never is when pigs fly, and yet I

have seen them soar in my every decade,
and who's to say, given what far-fetched
events have taken place in just one life,
that pigs will not fly farther, fly higher,
launch themselves into empyrean space?
I find the impossible is only improbable,
the merely unlikely almost to expect,
and fifty years from now, a hundred fifty,
why not, you—O Unknown Confidant—
may read this poem and have like ideas,
undisturbed by the herd of frolicking pigs
rising in ecstasy over your inclined head.

The Owl of Minerva

flies at dusk, says Hegel, although
I wouldn't know, not having seen it
or the wisdom it's meant to bring.
(Which is OK by me . . . if the deal
is *See Naples and Die*, well then
why would you want to see Naples?)
Other owls, I'm familiar with:
Tyto alba, for one, the ordinary
barn owl, its face like some visitor's
from outer space, its harsh cry
fit for a *banshee* with laryngitis.
I used to hear that jarring sound
while resisting slumber as a child,
sent off to bed in the long twilight
of a South Fork summer's eve
and waiting for the ghastly screech
to punctuate the lisp and sough
of Sagaponack's persistent wind
and interrupt the seaside pulse
of the breaking waves nearby.

You knew it was sure to come,
but it scared you all the same,
just as it startled cowering voles
and field mice that left their bones
bundled with their skin and teeth
in regurgitated pellets moldering
under a messy nest in our back yard.
Owl or *banshee*, the voice is said
to foretell death, and yet no one died
in our home till the birds had flown
elsewhere or were dead themselves,
and clearly, if anyone was called,
it wasn't me, who lived to grow up,

more or less, and move in my turn
to other fields and beds and houses
and the sound of other evenings.

What children hear at the edge
of dream reverberates in memory
to form a soundtrack for nostalgia,
echoes in their way more real
than the noise of every day, but
I'm hearing them again of late,
cries made by what my neighbors say
is the tawny owl (*Strix selvatica*)
inhabiting an abandoned limekiln
buried deep in the hillside woods
above our farm in Fiesole, a place
where summer sunsets delight
all creatures and shadows hunt
under olive trees as night comes on.
The collapsed kiln is the sort of ruin
Romantic poets invent when none
is handy, an old stone tower half-
returned to nature and no earthly use
to anyone unequipped with wings.
Its picturesque decay is no great
distance from our garden terrace,
and at the cocktail hour, I fill a glass
and take my seat and wait to see
the raptor climb into the fading light
to hover overhead as the air cools
down and the breeze picks up.

Stark against the sky and close
to motionless, its floating presence
takes me back. In time, my mother
had her coronary in our Sagaponack
home, though she was by then far
too deaf to hear any owl that might

have lingered there to call her name.
She certainly wouldn't hear this one,
its gentle hoot uneasy to distinguish
amid barks and howls and grunts
that animate a rural landscape rife
with many hungers. I'm aware of it
mostly in bed, as in years gone by,
waking again in the dark and needing
the bathroom or simply too restless
to sleep. The lone syllable it repeats
(perhaps just trying to get it right)
will never be mine to understand
(an owl's reason eludes our own),
but for the moment I'm not terribly
disturbed. If the cry in the night
has an object, who knows who
it might be, and these days I find
wisdom an increasingly nebulous
concept not soon to be identified
in beast or book . . . and anyway,
Hegel is someone I haven't read.

Those Were the Days

We were happy as pigs in whatever makes a pig happy.
We caught world-class nightcrawlers in the rise-and-shine, and the
    pinguid poultry was as much as we could handle.
Seamstresses back then were many and available and kept us in
    stitches any time.
It was all good as gold, whether it glittered or not.

We averted our eyes before we leapt, and we landed on our own two
    knees.
We took misunderstandings right out of each other's mouth.
Sure, we had needy acquaintances: some things don't change.
Our money insisted on a trial separation, and you'd feel foolish, too.

We proposed non-stop, but God was mostly indisposed.
We called all cookware colorless, to be on the safe side.
Clothes made the men and unmade the women, so everybody opted
    for T-shirts and cargo pants, and we grew to fit the container.
We used it up, we wore it out, we made it do, as do the trout.

A penny saved was half a cent.
We guzzled wine for auld lang syne and said the buzz was never better.
We lost the drum and kept on marching.
As a rule we were safe. In the end we were sorry anyway.

Drachenfutter

You're supposed to save some of each day
for poetry if you want your muse to favor you
with inspired verse (or even if you hope to tie
a few clumsy lines together), and I haven't, I've
strayed, been distracted, turning to any number
of essentially irrelevant pursuits: I took every drug
I could find (just for fun, I was lucky), I wrote
contemporary art reviews (an expense of spirit
in a waste of gallery space), I played at learning
foreign languages (I've yet to learn my own),
I played in a punk-rock band (only briefly, like
maybe ten minutes, but still . . .), and having
been so often so untrue, Darling, in my fashion,
what can I do to make amends now, when so much
seems smoke in the wind and poems are what's left?
Drachenfutter. Having run off with an exotic dancer,
or come home drunk and abused the maid, or gambled
away his wedding ring, or just forgotten an anniversary,
the apologetic German brings his *Frau* "dragon fodder,"
a dress, a diamond, a brand-new Mercedes Benz.
Alas, I can't afford such gifts, and if I could I like
to think no muse of mine would be quite so venal,
and moreover (though it just makes matters worse
if one points it out), she hasn't been perfect either,
she's wandered too, I might have used more help—
just look at the pages of evidence and you tell me.
Truth is, our affair has sometimes lacked pizzazz.
Truth is we've hurt each other and should have done
better, but I'm willing to forgive, or at least forget
(it's what humans do best), and bring what I can
to a *rapprochement* . . . my incorrigible innocence
almost untouched, my weakness for how she tickled
my fancy, nuzzled my ear, how she set my lips on fire,
the aching heart that is what I'm worth and finally
all I offer: shamefaced fodder for the dragon.

Digging Out

Not once a year, nor even two or three,
but once a decade now a single snow
falls in sufficient quantities to show
self-reliance is a fool's endeavor,
coating New England heavily as ever
in downy flakes so thick they can provoke
a heart attack or break the plow and keep
swamp Yankees trapped inside like city folk.
When snows of yesteryear lie round about
and walks and drives are loaded three feet deep
with drifts like those of childhood memory,
I don't mind asking help with digging out,
a task beyond the scope of one man's labors.
Sometimes even poets love their neighbors.

Wartime and After

I didn't go to the wars of my youth (I had several chances).
    I don't regret it, those who went regret it:
wars are forever acclaimed in the making, but rarely in hindsight,
    when parents weep and damaged men return
to a society bloodshed and suffering haven't improved much.
    Instead, I spent my twenties chasing women
(some of whom slowed down sufficiently that even I overtook them)
    and drinking wine, when good Bordeaux was cheap.

It's a cliché, but I sang a bit, too, although music was never
    my talent (sometimes dogs would leave the room);
what I was good at was poetry, odd as that is, and I studied
    the craft for years, its art so long to learn.
In the beginning, I couldn't appreciate poets who didn't
    compose the kind of verse I wrote myself,
call it Cavafy as filtered through Stevens. By now, I'm more open-
    minded but don't care the way I used to.

Lately the poets I read have been dead a long time, like Propertius
    and Horace, clever friends I meet each morning.
Evenings, I still like to savor the winemaker's art, though in portions
    less damaging than once. And as for women,
one day I found one I liked well enough to put up with for decades,
    patient, pretty, pretty smart, and she
seemed to be willing to tolerate me, so at last we got married.
    I gave up singing. No one has complained.

These days a pastime I favor is simply to stare out the window:
    our house is in the woods, so nature brings
parables drawn from the animal kingdom right up to our doorstep,
    and there is beauty in their grim detail.
Some of my recent poems tell of the struggles of sparrows and field mice,
    and I am not displeased with the results,
not that they win any medals. That's sensible. Medals are given
    to wines, to runners, soldiers home from war.

Yankee Spring

Up here, when apple trees begin to bloom,
that shed their petals on the ground like snow
and fill the air as if they filled a room
with hints of allspice and the fleeting scent
of clove, they start the season like a gun.

As iris buds, the bleeding-heart will grow,
the sparrow find its mate and build its nest,
the shad must run, the roe and milt be spent,
one squirrel chase another to and fro.
Spring has to race to get its business done

within the few weeks that it has to go
before the rising heat will have depressed
its urge and raising young take precedent,
and so each frantic creature chants its song:
I have to have you and we don't have long.

Love Poem

A mother's I don't remember, not that I didn't ingest it in infancy or
that she couldn't feel the instinctive attachment.
Still, her second husband was an attractive expedient, and I was an
article of agreement.
I bristled when she touched me, steeled myself at her approach, and
when she was living I couldn't relent, and when she was dead
naturally she couldn't, either.

My father and I loved each other unthinking, as dogs do their kennel
or salmon their stream, as people love the first landscape they
encounter.
I had words for everything in life but him, and I sat by in silence as
he shrank to nothing.
When he died I went into the bathroom and wept.

The amorous performances of teenage girls involved me as a
conscripted witness, the necessary audience in a theater of
the cruel.
Love was how blood leapt to glimpse a face, how thought winced to
recall a name.
It was an unforgiving contest whose ferocious rules I learned well
enough to get my innings in.

Love of a woman arrived unforeseen, an affection emerging when
the ice within me broke and flowed to some sea.
Woman's love drifted in and became as weather, a prevailing wind,
a private atmosphere.
Fair or foul, it was the climate, I couldn't imagine another.

Love of our child was well-prepared astonishment, its immediate
caring an abiding concern.
It was the harsh tactic of a heartless world, a stratagem that sapped
self-confidence as its imperiled object became my hostage
to Event.
I clutched the new love with tremulous hands, anxious ever after.

My other loves haven't required relatives or comprehended friends
  (both a comfort and obligation, those aren't lovers so much as
  members of a club).
The rest haven't even been personal (or if so, only from my side of
  each tempestuous affair).
My other lovers have been things, and I've had many, inanimate
  romances that were chance enchantments (not less precious
  for that).

—For a long while, I adored the ocean, living on and in it for decades,
  till one day we were finished: the seaside was just damp sand.
—A pilgrim searching out moderately obscure images in extremely
  obscure sanctuaries, I pursued Italian painting as a type of
  faith.
—Moved by hypothetical emotion to genuine tears, I shivered
  hearing the grand artifice of operatic arias.
—Gripped and fevered, I found myself possessed by the fleeting
  odors of French wine, the abraged shades of antique carpets,
  the other and orderly world that is the game of chess, the
  corporeal chess that can be the game of fencing.
—Above all, I devoted myself to language, giving it my deepest
  respect, my truest loyalty, my least feigned fascination.

I declare my loves to be no more arbitrary than anybody else's.
I attest I've been honest in my affections: I had no choice.
I perceive I've loved most what troubled me most, though if this was
  cause or effect I can't tell.

I feel my thirst for love has only increased with time.
I think, in the end, I shall love all my life.
I know it will never love me.

Shame and *Schadenfreude*

The kid who hit the line drive that struck
me in the face as I pitched softball and then
stood over my childish tears amid a group
of older boys and told me to toughen up
was drafted soon after and died in Viet Nam.

The woman who cleaned our house and had
my affection until the day she discovered
pornographic books beneath my mattress
and took them away to show my mother
suffered for years before cancer killed her.

The schoolmate who saw me masturbating
in a bathroom and circulated the story
throughout the Dickensian institution
where I was sent for my education will see
no more reunions following his heart attack.

The heavily muscled but poorly socialized
town delinquent who often threatened to beat
me bloody and one time did became addicted
to heroin and was arrested for selling the same
and eventually succumbed to AIDS in prison.

The knowledgeable girl who to my surprise
had occasion to judge me clumsy in bed
and preferred scorn to any effort to teach
later married an abusive husband, so that I
was almost sorry to hear of her car accident.

The slush-pile reader at a third-rate journal
who never showed my work to a senior editor
but sent rejections noting grammatical errors
appeared in his brief obituary recently, and I
struggled to feel anything but *Schadenfreude*.

I survived them all, the humiliators, all I recall,
though surely there were others, given how
fugitive even painful memories are, and though
surely more await me, given how notorious
for its mortifications the process of aging is.

Still, I've outlived it so far, the embarrassment,
the indignity, the loss of pride, the loss of face,
all the chagrin of ineptitude and ignorance,
and for years I'd hoped to savor the triumph
but find myself oddly diminished instead,

as if each agent of abasement now expired,
each bitter episode now finally put paid,
had taken some essential part of me with it
and left me weaker, untethered, ill defined,
somehow less human if less ashamed.

One Substance

The old dog shivers, trying to stand, and I think
of my father shivering in flannel pajamas under
a bundle of blankets on Long Island in September,
who was born before World War I and died
with the American century one year almost
to the day before the Towers came down and ash
turned the tip of Manhattan into a vision of Pompeii.
The dog shudders, falls, struggles to find its feet.
Love and loss are so intertwined some days I don't
even dream I might look back to tell them apart.

An Argument with Reason

Come, my Reason, why can't we be friends
since each upon the other much depends?
You'll never analyze your mortal case
when it has ceased to occupy its space,
and nothing I invent will last for long
if what I write is puzzled out all wrong.
Thus for the present you adhere to me,
whereas my prospects of posterity
seem stuck with you, and let us not fall out
precisely when that future is in doubt:
working to shake off a vague malaise,
I fear we both have seen our better days,
and it's my guess it won't be long before
the two of us don't quibble anymore;
so for a while, before it comes to that,
why don't we entertain ourselves and chat?
They named an era for you years ago
before mankind knew all it cares to know,
an age in which it was no shame to learn
and thought expended was its own return,
when print was not the opposite of leisure,
hours were books, and people read for pleasure,
when careless usage was not paradigm
and eloquence not tantamount to crime,
an organized, precise, coherent time
preceding Blake and after Henry Vaughan,
before our industry had come and gone
and the Communication Age began
to discombobulate attention span.
Contemporary authors, who confuse
all yesterday with yesterday's old news,
too lazy, too caught up, or too harassed
to take a passing interest in the past,
the notions that they have no time to think
heaped in their heads like dishes in a sink

as pixeled screens distract them from pursuit
of any happiness that won't compute,
might well, if they could quit their video,
remember d'Alembert and Diderot.
What would society look like today
if such men were not moved to *raisonner*?
What would our job description be at present?
A span of years spent swinking as a peasant.
Had mind and independence never met,
aristocrats might drive their plowmen yet:
condemned to decades miserably fed,
despised alive and soon forgot when dead,
a beast at best, a heretic at worst,
baptized at birth and ever after cursed
as born too low, then threatened by the priest
with fire forever when the serfdom ceased,
the common man would be no better off
but for the efforts of the *philosophe*.

   Not so fast, you say (for sceptic Reason
has discontent enough for every season,
and no complaint can be so recondite
as to escape inspection by its light),
thought and thought applied are not the same.
The epoch masquerading in my name
owes its credit but has earned its blame,
the credit due to Paine or to Voltaire,
the blame a dividend on profit share,
since savage indignation is a fee
paid swiftly if it buys prosperity.
Enlightenment was largely an excuse
for exploitation, grapeshot, and the noose,
and rationality could close its eyes
when used as rationale to colonize.
Was zealous superstition offered check?
Maybe in Ferney, but not Quebec.
Did European values cross the waves?

Well, yes, if what you meant was trading slaves.
The Eighteenth Century, for all its wits,
might well be called the Age of Hypocrites,
since it's mere fashion that makes much of sense
when most conclusion is a sheer pretense.
The Chain of Being wasn't so abstract
that coffles didn't form a chain in fact,
and men back then imagined nothing new:
the whip for many, Reason for the few.

But almost any century can be
accused of crimes against humanity
(so idle questions form their own reply
when doubts about themselves intensify)
while those that manage to progress are much
more rare and should be recognized as such.
Whatever guilt revisionists attach
to prior time and place could be no match
for ours, not after all the times we've tried
to modernize our world with genocide.
You can't compare the carnage then with now!
Would any but a backward age allow
the Great Leap Forward made by Chairman Mao?
Would any but a Frankfurt School old-timer
still referencing Adorno and Horkheimer
believe the Eighteenth Century at fault
for Stalin's labor camps or Buchenwald?
For bigoted fanatics who mistreat
their masses, bygone zealots can't compete
with those we've seen; and if it's money made
from misery you want, well I'm afraid
the international narcotics trade
puts any other commerce in the shade:
was profiting from slaves more inhumane
than dealing heroin or crack cocaine?
Besides, albeit mostly for the bed,
slaves still exist: the difference is, instead

of chaining Africans to frigate decks,
we traffic Filipina girls for sex.
Yet I will grant you the Enlightenment
perfected every evil men invent,
if you will grant me that with all its sins,
it's where the unencumbered mind begins.
Jefferson's ideas are not diminished
because our need for them is never finished.

    Let's put the proposition in reverse:
admit the modern era isn't worse
than many that preceded it and add
it offers more than any we have had.
Populations now are much more free
than any people known to history:
free to have opinions, free to share
their wild ideas with anyone they care,
free to congregate, and free to lust
whatever way their bodies say they must.
The internet you're eager to deplore
brings a world's acquaintance to your door
and carries you to destinations which
were once for felons only, or the rich.
The globe lies waiting at your fingertips,
and for old-fashioned visits, planes and ships
that make the most exotic ports of call
require mere modicums of wherewithal:
this age is when all distances grew small.
If evil's with us always, as you state,
then it solves nothing to commiserate,
and dwelling on the problems that persist
through every age ignores what gains exist
in ours alone—say half the earth's deprived
of food and dignity and has survived
by suffering, that still leaves billions who
have more to eat and drink and think and do
than ever—just do the arithmetic!—

to wallow in nostalgia makes me sick.
And what about our medical advances?
If you went back in time and took your chances,
the chances are the feverish result
is that you'd die before you were adult,
since doctors then met physical distress
with leeches rather than with cleanliness,
and public hygiene was still incomplete
without an open sewer in the street.
You conjure virtues, praising an ideal
past at the expense of what is real
right now, the way a codger wipes his eyes
for faded oceans or departed skies,
as if it were a badge of intellect
to denigrate the present and detect
some sort of moral turpitude beneath
our longer lives and better-looking teeth;
but once the bargain asked was understood,
who would trade such comforts if he could?
The world right now has never been so good.

There have been gains, but look at what we've lost!
And comforts, too, but comforts at what cost?
The problems we encounter make one gasp,
and earth has changed so much it's hard to grasp;
to think, where George the Third once played at farming
our Heads of State contend with global warming.
You laugh about a changing sky and sea
as if they represent eternity,
when fishing boats the Japanese equipped
with nets the size of Tokyo have stripped
our oceans bare, and when the ozone hole
we've punctured over the Antarctic pole
threatens to transform our atmosphere
into an outlook anything but clear,
till now the only forecast that is sure
is that the world we've fashioned can't endure.

Why, we're already waking to the ills
of carbon footprints and their monthly bills;
we're adding ethanol to gasoline
so our exhaust might qualify as green;
we're keeping our discarded plastic hidden
down at the bottom of the public midden;
we're pressuring our Congress to demand
what business climate climate can withstand
and just how much ecology it takes
a tax return to qualify for breaks;
and now we have so prudently begun
conserving, by the time we've had our fun
who's to say what harm we won't have done,
and if it won't require some sacrifice
of living standard with the glacial ice?
The point is, creature comforts aren't forever
nor in themselves a cultural endeavor
worthy of the name. It's not what things
an age accumulates, but what it brings
to mind that counts, the impact of its thought,
seeing as the tender flesh it sought
to clothe and cosset, or at minimum
defend and feed throughout its tiny sum
of days, has given up its struggle, while
ideas it had of how to reconcile
fact with dream, reality with hope,
the cynicism of the misanthrope
with all the altruistic self-restraint
and humble disposition of a saint,
are mostly what an era may bequeath
to those who follow after and will breathe
the like beliefs and self-same molecules
of air exhaled by *philosophes* and fools
for generations past. Who cares what kind
of toilet seat our ancestors designed,
how their odor issues were controlled,
what steps they took to treat a common cold?

How they kept their winter chilblains warm
is not what interests; it's how they inform
us still. And maybe they were wise to freeze,
since too much comfort is its own disease!
I worry that the gains of which we speak
will leave us stupid as they make us weak,
and that our Need to Know degrades to whim
as our experience becomes less grim
than what it was before the latest science
sapped our leisured age of self-reliance.
Convenience flattens out the learning curve.
Just turn your TV on and you'll observe
the facile way our ignorance is shared
in bite-sized pieces of illusion aired.
We questioned deeper when our lives were tough,
and comfy minds don't ponder hard enough.

It won't surprise you that I disagree.
Leisure's naught but opportunity
and can be wasted as it can be used
to good result. The people most enthused
by hardship not infrequently were raised
without it, just as labor's often praised
by those for whom the prospect is remote
that they will be obliged to lift and tote.
Moreover, toughness rarely is outdated
but rather often highly overrated.
The moral fiber hardihood comes with
resembles heroism, mostly myth:
we only find it in the past because
such virtue never is but always was.
Of me, you could observe as much as well,
that Reason is a tale one age will tell
another and is seldom how it looks
on cenotaphs or in old history books,
where fabulists like Gibbon may define
a thousand years of empire as decline

and thereby follow what was Livy's lead
in situating all courageous deed
and every lucid thought in misty regions
unseen by any but the Roman legions.
It's not surprising scholars are impressed
by olden days: it's what they know the best.
They find their subjects worthy by default,
but take their findings with a grain of salt,
because if all your wisdom is received,
you haven't thought so much as you believed.
The Eighteenth Century can make one laugh
that never pleaded on its own behalf
but for its first appeal and last resort
adduced antiquity in its support,
imagining, like you, that rigor kept
our forebears less corrupt and more adept
in argument than we who still may fail
the test of character our lives entail.
Yet is it likely with the march of years
the Nature of the Species disappears?
Or that the human heart can be outgrown?
That men once knew what still cannot be known?
Is compromised integrity perhaps
not always cause for cultural collapse?
By now we've learned our destinies are linked
more to the savagery and greed instinct
in us than to some parabolic arc
of rise and fall that leaves men in the dark.
The key to fate is in the chromosome,
not in the decadence of ancient Rome.

Yes and no. The genes you're thinking of
are limits difficult to rise above,
but fall we do . . . why, instances abound
of cultures that dramatically lose ground,
and what is learned is readily forgot.
The Middle Ages happened, did they not?

Go check your atlas if you want the proof
of what we sink to once the civic roof
caves in—it makes one wince to look upon
such former garden spots as Lebanon,
Kashmir, Ceylon, Cambodia, and Laos
and the speed with which we cede to chaos
when social structure twists all out of joint
and ruthlessness has reached the tipping point.
Since barbarism often overwhelms
us to this day, to travel in the realms
of gold and silver ages long destroyed
is not to live in dreamland or avoid
the present—it is not to disregard
precedent or shrink from what is hard.
And if the *philosophes* are always apt
to quote the classics, they aren't simply trapped
within the past. You ought to credit them
with better sense. It was a stratagem
of flank attack: the centuries B.C.
let them circumvent theology.
Antique approval licensed their research
in volumes that a Censor of the Church
might not admire but couldn't well forbid,
since they were doing what Aquinas did,
who saw his fine distinctions would increase
the more he cited texts from Ancient Greece.
The *philosophes* had other aims, of course,
and they used Aristotle as their source
for concepts sainted authors don't endorse,
like noting things that actually occur
on earth instead of all we must infer
of heaven, which profound respect for what
is real became an instrument to cut
the tangled web of faith; and with the yoke
of dogma thrown, why let god-fearing folk
reattach the traces? If we braved
such superstition once, why have we caved

into it now? Our culture stands indicted
of an unseemly haste to be benighted
once again. The element you miss
in your historical analysis
is the existential cowardice
that marks our time. A satirist could weep
at how we've put irreverence to sleep,
especially where our poetry's concerned:
today approval's prized and laughter's spurned,
and who will write a couplet that confronts
absurdity with ridicule as once
was standard literary practice? Our
poets have grown too polite to shower
obscurantism with amused contempt,
although a versifier's not exempt
in turn from being treated to the scorn
which those awaiting Armageddon's morn
and hoping to achieve a state of grace
that no amount of Reason can erase
reserve for "humanists," which I conceive
means you and me, and let's not be naïve,
we shouldn't be restrained by etiquette
from recognizing an eternal threat
to all that we hold sacred, like free speech
and bonded bourbon, when the godly preach
the Gospel, blowing smoke to form the fog
of nonsense precious to the mystagogue.
On any given Sunday, incensed clerics
exhort the credulous into hysterics
and use such energy for all its worth
to institute their Kingdom Come on earth.
They profit from a weakness of the flesh,
that stale beliefs so often pass for fresh:
the tale may be bizarre, the logic skewed,
the quoted scripture wildly misconstrued,
but mumbo-jumbo dating to the dawn
of Man lives on, its magic never gone,

its spell recast in hocus-pocus which
is altered just enough to find its niche . . .
so does the ancient mystery cult emerge
to surface as some sainted demiurge,
and newly minted liturgies are coined
in Californian communes from purloined
writ and pseudo-scientific theory.
The vigor of unreason makes me weary,
and if I see the visionary gleam
in one more pair of eyes I think I'll scream.
When you consider what has since transpired,
your unbowed era has to be admired
that uttered its derision right out loud
and owned the outrage and would not be cowed.

　　You sound a bit worked up yourself. Relax,
religion is immune to such attacks.
Only innocents desire the truth,
and outrage is a luxury of youth.
Whatever ails your versifiers can't
be treated by descending into rant,
and there aren't many poets who can cope
with dunces as did Alexander Pope.
Besides, you ought to see the truth he saw,
that laughter is no substitute for law,
not least the laws of nature. If the key
to psychological stability
is recognizing what can't be improved,
then to be content you'd be behooved
to face the fact we rarely have the strength
required to view the void at any length,
and given life's a meaningless and nonce
event, delusion is a sane response.
Confirmed agnostics have been known to put
their faith in charms and keep a rabbit's foot,
and even atheists will sometimes cross
their fingers or be careful where they toss

the salt, because if fantasy's a crutch,
a crutch is sorely needed: life's too much
to live with minus magic, and in brief,
most people can't get by without belief.
The Eighteenth Century was mad, that dreamed
this world could be detailed and thus redeemed
by fact from longing for the Great Beyond,
as if the evidence could correspond
to implicated thought, that crazy quilt
we patch together out of fear and guilt
and hope, the homespun motley of our lives,
a winding sheet wherein the self survives
to be a gleaming ray or tortured wraith
in the mirage oasis seen by faith.
When all is said and done, what else is left
of us except the twisted warp and weft
of our invention? What escapes the worm
if not the complex metaphor you term
a tangled web? And isn't it the précis
we call the Word that typifies the species?
Religion sets humanity apart
as much as humor does or making art,
and if activity creates the creature,
then piety is our defining feature—
a leopard has its spots, a zebra stripes,
and we have gods, for all that wisdom gripes.
Verse and atheism, too, are types
of credence, shapes dubiety assumes
the while we wait in one of Stevens' Rooms
or stanzas, disciplines that we adopt
arbitrarily, the way we opt
to practice any habit of the tribe
cognition can devise or pen describe:
to lose an accent and reject the voice
we started with before we had a choice,
to seek society and join the club
and smile at people we would rather snub,

to tire of catered meals and learn to cook
and suffer indigestion by the book,
to close uneasiness within a clause
and grasp at form the way we clutch at straws.
The soul's election verges on caprice
yet who's to say it will not give us peace,
who only need a story line involved
to feel our sorrow eased and problems solved.
With or without the benefit of clergy,
people gravitate to thaumaturgy,
and it is just this impulse that's displaced
into the rhetoric that suits your taste.
What priests call holy and the poets weird
has lapsed of late but never disappeared,
and to this day, most poetry employs
more of the numinous than it destroys.
Language fit to decorate an altar
has been the object ever since the Psalter,
and finally it amounts to little odds
if one verse mumbles or another nods,
the best of lines will always show a bias
for phrases raised enough to pass for pious.
The perfect pitch of the Augustan age
elevates the diction of its page
to strike a tone by which its authors climbed
above the obstacle of how they rhymed,
and what except sublimity could lift
the end-stopped lines of Johnson, Gay, or Swift?
As for the mockery that you desire
preached to your humanists as to a choir,
it rarely takes a lowly effort higher,
since purple passages are hard to craft
once the Muse has reached her crux and laughed.
Pointed verses are more dull than sharp
if all they illustrate is how to carp,
and there's no artifice that can afford
to have its lack of purpose underscored.

What you call satire was the fear of change,
a kneejerk disapproval of the strange,
the bitter jests of cowards who had dared
to look into the future and despaired.
Besides, most poets then were not agnostic
but were at once canonical and caustic.
Encyclopaedists were the ones afflicted
with the enlightened views that you've depicted,
and there's no reasoning that is not flawed
if it's beside the point, so why applaud
a project history has revealed as fraud?
Irreligion is a waste of breath,
and satire is a genre done to death.

   Have cognitive psychologists explained
why your recalcitrance is so ingrained?
I started out to praise your Age, and couldn't
utter anything with which you wouldn't
find some fault. Does there exist a field
in which your urge to contradict will yield?
It's enough to drive us all berserk
contemplating Reason's handiwork,
that pours its criticism in our cup
and smiles as we attempt to drink it up,
that adds its tart corrective to those dregs
and never hears a theory but it begs
to differ. It's not argument to bicker
and not dispositive to glance and snicker,
and opposition is not dialectic
if all it is in essence is dyspeptic.
We educate ourselves to undertake
a life of contemplation for your sake,
and learn when it's too late that we misjudged
the likely recompense the while we drudged,
as by and by your niggling comes to spoil
our sense of satisfaction in the toil.
I hoped the Age of Reason might instruct

an author yet in how to best conduct
the enterprise of art, that its adroit
metrics might be something to exploit,
and that the light it shed might still illumine
what it means to be alive and human;
I now begin to think your Age was smug
responding to soul-searching with a shrug,
and that your wisdom is a manner born
of common sense combined with practiced scorn.
Worse, I've got to say suspicion mounts
that Reason won't stand by us when it counts,
that when we ask you for assistance we
will meet with nonstop ambiguity
and hear analysis without conviction
it will ever winnow fact from fiction.
Your dramas of distinction are a farce,
since most of what they teach us is to parse
your name as predicate and not as noun,
as process not as thing, a way to drown
in circumstance. But circumstances don't
arrive at substance if their details won't
cohere. In life or art, it was absurd
to think your discourse might enhance my word.

In your sixth decade, you act surprised
at what I am, as if you realized
only today that I would just as soon
fall silent as be made to sing your tune.
A million shades of meaning round you swirled,
and you hoped I would harmonize your world?
I know a thing or two, or even three,
but I can't promise you concinnity.

Years go by, and neither of us knows
the heart and soul of poetry or prose,
so tell me, where to turn for help with those?

Study your confusion and compose.

A Stroll in the Rain

When I was a boy and weekdays walked my mile
      to school and, I like to say, two miles coming home,
      no child was sent out into precipitation without some
serious protection, a garb like hazmat gear, juvenile
versions of a style suited to the Grand Banks: bright
      canary-yellow slickers, and Gloucester hats as well,
      and galoshes that looked like seaman's boots and fell
heavily as stones as we stomped in puddles in spite
of admonitions not to get wet and catch our deaths.
      Back then even grownups, if there was the merest
      hint of rain, went no place at all, not to the nearest
store and certainly not to work, without latex sheaths
in their attachés that could encase their shiny leather
      shoes in coverings known by a name that did not refer
      only to what discouraged pregnancy or a rain of fire
upon the privates, but to what kept off bad weather.

The times keep changing. In the *settecento* Veneto,
      when the hottest painter was an undemonstrative
      practitioner of a style once dismissed as decorative
and now much admired, Giovanni Battista Tiepolo,
the damp local climate was never seen on ceilings
      of the ancestral villas he and his son filled with swirls
      of cloud holding graybeard men and pink-skinned girls
clad in light and silk alone, raiment typically revealing
widely spaced, petite breasts below hair piled high
      in elaborate coifs dressed in pearls, and neither satin
      nor braid nor an aged hand giving a gentle pat on
a naked hip are ever anything but confidently dry,
in spite of *acqua alta* and the Brenta in autumn spate
      and the unabated inundation of disastrous news
      regarding political decline and revolutionary views
that assailed *La Serenissima*'s no longer stable state.

If you like your figures more realistic and less static,
        albeit fully clothed and thus in the end less fetching,
        consider a mysterious series of undated etchings
by Giandomenico, the son, of which the most enigmatic
is a promenade sometimes titled *A Stroll in the Rain.*
        The rain in question is just a sprinkle, and the stroll
        at best an amble, an almost aimless drift of seven souls
towards a grove of trees they are in no hurry to gain.
It looks to be a family outing: man, woman, and child,
        their three servants, and say a friend, walk with faces
        hidden, their backs to us, proceeding at a stately pace
while a bored dog with nothing to chase stands in profile
giving us the only eye we see. No one has ever explained
        why one retainer is dressed as Punch, and no one knows
        why sunless shadows fall or where everybody's supposed
to be going. Something called. They went. It rained.

ACKNOWLEDGMENTS

Various of the poems here selected from previous books first appeared in the following publications: *Antaeus, Grand Street, The Hartford Courant, New England Review,* the *New Republic,* the *Paris Review, Partisan Review, Poetry, Shenandoah, Southwest Review, Standpoint, Verse, Western Humanities Review,* and the *Yale Review.* The poems "Christ Pantocrator in San Giorgio dei Greci," "*Nostalgie de la Boue,*" "Millrace," "A Scrap of Sky," and "In an Old Garden" first ran in the *New Yorker.*

"Negative Space" first appeared in the *American Scholar;* "The Old Country" first appeared in the *Antioch Review;* "Wartime and After" and "One Substance" first appeared in *Literary Imagination;* "A Stroll in the Rain" first appeared in *The New Criterion.* "What a Dog Wouldn't Eat" first appeared in the *New Republic;* "Penicillin and the Anthropocene Apocalypse" first appeared in the *Paris Review;* "How the Forest Was Disenchanted" and "Those Were the Days" first appeared in *Raritan;* "Cattywumpus, Arfybarsed, Whopperjawed" first appeared in the *Yale Review;* "An Argument with Reason" first appeared as a chapbook published by Sea Cliff Press; "The Owl of Minerva" first appeared (as "*La nottola di Minerva*") in *Almanacco* (It.), and I thank the enormously skilled Simone Dubrovic for his splendid translation. "Those Were the Days" also appeared in *The Best American Poetry, 2018,* edited by David Lehman and Dana Gioia.

Stanza breaks obscured by pagination are intended at the bottom of these pages: 5, 13, 41, 45, 47, 69, 114, 138, 170, 172, and 190.

ABOUT THE AUTHOR

George Bradley is the author of five previous books of verse published by Yale University Press, Knopf, and The Waywiser Press. His first collection won the Yale Younger Poets Prize, and he is the editor of *The Yale Younger Poets Anthology* (1998). Among the other awards his poetry has received are the Witter Bynner Prize from the American Academy and Institute of Arts and Letters, the Peter I. B. Lavan Award from the Academy of American Poets, and a grant from the National Endowment for the Humanities. Bradley's work has appeared in many magazines (*The New Yorker*, the *New Republic*, *Poetry*, *Parnassus*, the *Paris Review*, and others) as well as a wide variety of anthologies, and poems of his have often been selected for the annual *The Best American Poetry* volumes. He has read at venues around the country, among them the Library of Congress in Washington, D.C., the 92nd St. "Y" in New York, and the Lannan Foundation, then in Los Angeles.

Bradley has been variously employed as a construction worker, a sommelier, an editor, and a copywriter. At present, he imports and distributes a brand of extra virgin olive oil (*La Bontà di Fiesole*) produced on a farm in Tuscany. When not on the farm, he lives in Chester, near the river of rivers in Connecticut.